→ **INTRODUCING**

BERTRAND RUSSELL

DAVE ROBINSON & JUDY GROVES

Published in the UK in 2011
by Icon Books Ltd,
Omnibus Business Centre,
39–41 North Road,
London N7 9DP
email: info@iconbooks.co.uk
www.introducingbooks.com

Sold in the UK, Europe,
South Africa and Asia
by Faber & Faber Ltd,
Bloomsbury House,
74–77 Great Russell Street,
London WC1B 3DA
or their agents

Distributed in the UK, Europe,
South Africa and Asia
by TBS Ltd,
TBS Distribution Centre,
Colchester Road,
Frating Green,
Colchester CO7 7DW

This edition published in Australia
in 2011 by Allen & Unwin Pty Ltd,
PO Box 8500, 83 Alexander Street,
Crows Nest, NSW 2065

Previously published in the UK and
Australia in 2002 under the current title

This edition published in the USA
in 2011 by Totem Books
Inquiries to: Icon Books Ltd,
Omnibus Business Centre,
39–41 North Road,
London N7 9DP, UK

Distributed to the trade in the USA
by Consortium Book Sales
and Distribution
The Keg House
34 Thirteenth Avenue NE, Suite 101,
Minneapolis, MN 55413-1007

Distributed in Canada
by Penguin Books Canada,
90 Eglinton Avenue East, Suite 700,
Toronto, Ontario M4P 2Y3

ISBN: 978-184831-302-6

Originating editor: Richard Appignanesi

Printed by Gutenberg Press, Malta

Russell, the Militant Philosopher

Everyone has heard of Bertrand Russell. He was a great thinker, an agitator imprisoned for his beliefs, and a man who changed Western philosophy for ever. He was a profound sceptic who refused to take anything for granted and protested all his life – against the senseless slaughter of the First World War, against the evils of all kinds of totalitarian dictatorship, and against nuclear weapons which he thought would eventually destroy us all. He wrote on a huge range of subjects and his work has influenced large numbers of people – from stuffy academics to scruffy anarchists.

"IF A MAJORITY IN EVERY CIVILIZED COUNTRY SO DESIRED, WE COULD, WITHIN 20 YEARS, ABOLISH ALL ABJECT POVERTY, QUITE HALF THE ILLNESS IN THE WORLD, THE WHOLE ECONOMIC SLAVERY WHICH BINDS DOWN NINE TENTHS OF OUR POPULATION; WE COULD FILL THE WORLD WITH BEAUTY AND JOY, AND SECURE THE REIGN OF UNIVERSAL PEACE."

Russell's Upbringing

Bertrand Russell was born in 1872 into a famous and wealthy English aristocratic family. His father was Viscount Amberley and his grandfather was the retired Prime Minister, Lord John Russell. England's most famous philosopher at that time, **John Stuart Mill** (1806-73), was his agnostic "Godfather". His parents were radical supporters of the Liberal Party and both advocated votes for women. They were shadowy figures in his life because his mother died of diphtheria when he was two and his father of bronchitis shortly afterwards. His main memories of childhood were of his grandmother, Lady Russell, and the oppressive atmosphere in her house – Pembroke Lodge in Richmond Park.

Bertie and his elder brother Frank were rigorously educated to be upstanding young gentlemen with a strong sense of religious and social duty. Neither boy was encouraged to think or talk about his dead, radical parents. Lady Russell also insisted that both boys receive regular lectures on personal conduct and avoid all talk of sexuality and bodily functions. Frank finally rebelled against his grandmother, but Bertie simulated obedience and, as a result, became a rather isolated, lonely and inauthentic child, acting out his grandmother's image of the perfectly obedient "angel".

THE MOST VIVID PART OF MY EXISTENCE WAS SOLITARY... THROUGHOUT MY CHILDHOOD I HAD AN INCREASING SENSE OF LONELINESS. I SELDOM MENTIONED MY MORE SERIOUS THOUGHTS TO OTHERS, AND WHEN I DID I REGRETTED IT. IT BECAME SECOND NATURE TO ME TO THINK THAT WHATEVER I WAS DOING HAD BETTER BE KEPT TO MYSELF.

Fear of Madness

It was a feeling of alienation that Russell found hard to shake off. He often felt like a "ghost" – unreal and insubstantial compared to other people. He had nightmares of being trapped behind a pane of glass, excluded for ever from the rest of the human race. He was also terrified of going mad. His uncle Willy was incarcerated in an asylum (for murdering a tramp in a workhouse infirmary) and his maiden Aunt Agatha was mentally unstable.

MY GRANDMOTHER TOLD ME...

IT WOULD BE UNWISE FOR YOU TO HAVE ANY CHILDREN, AS THEY WOULD ALSO PROBABLY BE DERANGED.

Many of Russell's friends and colleagues found him wonderfully amusing and compelling, but also strangely lacking in human warmth. His early days in Pembroke Lodge may have had a negative influence on his ability to relate to others, as well as explaining his powerful feelings of isolation.

The Geometry Lesson

Russell was educated privately by a series of often bizarre and eccentric tutors. (One did experiments on "imprinting" baby chickens, which consequently followed him all around the house.) Frank decided that it was time to teach his 11-year-old brother some geometry. It was a formative experience for Russell.

A Pure and Perfect World

It certainly looks as if Russell's brain was uniquely "wired up" for mathematical reasoning from an early age. But there was a problem. Like all knowledge systems, Euclidean geometry begins with a few "axioms" – statements that you just have to accept as true. ("A straight line is the shortest distance between two points." "All right angles are equal to one another.") The pragmatic Frank explained that it is impossible to generate a body of certain knowledge out of thin air. You have to start somewhere. But young Bertie had deep reservations.

HE WANTED GEOMETRY TO BE BEAUTIFULLY PERFECT AND TOTALLY TRUE.

PERHAPS THERE IS A WAY OF PROVING THE FOUNDATIONS OF GEOMETRY?

Mathematics offered Russell a pure and perfect world into which he could escape – a world that he spent much of his early life attempting to make even more perfect and true than it already was. Then, one of his well-informed private tutors told Russell of the existence of newly discovered alternative "non-Euclidean" geometries.

THESE ALSO WORK PERFECTLY WELL, EVEN THOUGH THEY ARE BASED ON WHOLLY DIFFERENT SETS OF AXIOMS.

THE UNIVERSE, AND THE SPACE OF WHICH IT IS MADE, IS NOT NECESSARILY "EUCLIDEAN".

So perhaps the young Bertie had been right to withhold his assent to Euclidean geometry after all.

9

The Quest For Reason

Russell subsequently came to believe that **reason** was the best way to solve all sorts of problems, not just mathematical ones. It was a view that he held for the rest of his life. He soon came to realize that the people he knew (his grandmother especially) maintained all sorts of beliefs that they could not justify. Russell soon began to have severe doubts about his own religious beliefs, and to experience feelings of sexual desire.

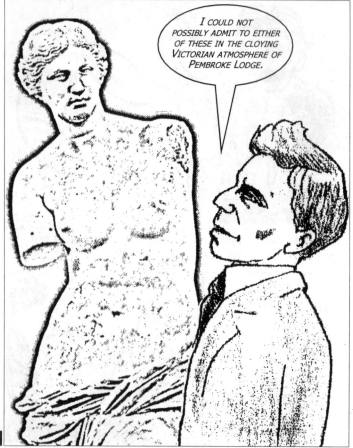

But even though he gradually lost all of his Christian faith, Russell remained a deeply spiritual individual. Much of his life seems to have been an almost spiritual quest for understanding and certainty. Sometimes he found it in his academic work. Sometimes he searched for it in the form of a perfect human companion who would totally comprehend him and so expel his constant feelings of isolation. Russell was also a prodigious and energetic walker, loved wild places and was, at times, a bit of a nature mystic.

Free at Last...

As soon as he arrived at Cambridge University, Russell felt intellectually liberated. He could talk openly at last about everything – mathematics, metaphysics, theology, politics, history – and make numerous friendships. He was soon invited to join the "Apostles" – an exclusive debating society made up of intellectually élitist young men. Here he met **G.E. Moore** (1873-1958), another great English philosopher-to-be.

13

The Platonist View of Mathematics

Russell impressed everyone with his mathematical mind. He was "Seventh Wrangler" in mathematics, and emerged with a "starred first" which enabled him to become a Fellow of Trinity College on graduating. By this time, his interest in mathematics was almost wholly theoretical and philosophical. This inevitably happens to anyone who starts to think about mathematics seriously. You soon find yourself asking some very odd questions – which make you into a philosopher.

IS MATHEMATICS SOMETHING MYSTERIOUSLY JUST "OUT THERE" IN THE UNIVERSE WAITING FOR US TO DISCOVER IT?

THIS IS WHAT PYTHAGORAS AND PLATO THOUGHT. BOTH BELIEVED THAT MATHEMATICS IS SOMEHOW "ENCODED" INTO THE UNIVERSE.

The Reality of Numbers

Many other philosophers, including Russell, agreed with Plato's idea that numbers are "real". But this view leads to strange problems about numbers. If numbers are "out there", how are they?

ARE THEY REAL IN THE WAY THAT DOGS AND SAUCEPANS ARE — OR ARE THEY REAL IN A DIFFERENT SORT OF WAY?

NUMBERS ARE "MORE REAL" THAN EVERYDAY OBJECTS.

Other philosophers, like Russell, maintained that numbers have an odd kind of "being" but not "existence", in the same way as some other entities do – like relations: "To the left of", "bigger than", etc.

The Formalist View

Some philosophers and mathematicians, usually known as "Formalists", claim that mathematics is a wholly human invention that is simply a construction of all that follows from a few axioms.

MATHEMATICS IS MERELY A KIND OF EMPTY GAME, LIKE CHESS, WITH CERTAIN RULES AND CONVENTIONS.

IT CANNOT TELL YOU ANYTHING ABOUT TRUTH, REALITY OR HOW THE UNIVERSE IS CONSTRUCTED, ALTHOUGH IT MAY PRODUCE VERY USEFUL "MODELS" OF WHAT THE UNIVERSE MIGHT BE LIKE.

Platonists think that mathematicians are uncovering the truth, Formalists that they are constructing interesting self-contained patterns that may eventually have some kind of practical application.

Three Kinds of Knowledge

Human beings can do mathematics in their minds without having to inspect the world. We can deduce that 2+2 = 4 without having to go outside and count dogs or saucepans.

PHILOSOPHERS CALL THIS **A PRIORI** KNOWLEDGE.

Some philosophers and mathematicians believe that mathematics can give us very real and new information about the world.

PHILOSOPHERS CALL THIS **SYNTHETIC** KNOWLEDGE.

Others insist that mathematics is merely "tautological" – it just repeats itself and is essentially empty. 2+2 = 4 is no more than 1+1+1+1 = 1+1+1+1.

PHILOSOPHERS CALL THIS **ANALYTIC** KNOWLEDGE.

Most philosophers and mathematicians agree that mathematics is "necessary" – the truth of it is constant, wherever and whenever. So 2+2 always equals 4, no matter where or when you live.

THIS KIND OF GUARANTEED TRUTH HAS ALWAYS ATTRACTED PHILOSOPHERS – AND IT WAS THIS MAGIC OF CERTAINTY THAT CAPTIVATED ME.

Mathematics may be the only really useful tool that we have if we are to investigate the deep structures of the universe, perhaps only because our minds are "wired up" to think mathematically. And this, in turn, raises yet more questions about the universe and the human minds that try to understand it.

Against Idealism

When Russell arrived at Cambridge, the "Idealist" philosophy of **F.H. Bradley** (1846-1924) held sway. Idealist philosophy claims that, if you are to understand the world and all that it contains, you have to recognize that everything is interconnected, and that separateness and contradictions are mere illusions. Idealist philosophers can find themselves in the end wallowing in a mystical vision of a harmonious whole, the "Absolute". The universe and its contents are all one thing.

FOR SOME IDEALIST PHILOSOPHERS, THIS "ONE THING" IS SOMETHING VERY LIKE GOD.

BRADLEY'S ARGUMENTS ARE OFTEN WELL-FORMULATED AND EXTREMELY PERSUASIVE.

BUT BOTH G.E. MOORE AND I THOUGHT THAT BRADLEY WAS WRONG.

Moore was a "common sense" sceptic who refused to accept weird philosophical conclusions, however well argued. Russell thought that analysis, not synthesis, was the only reliable way to arrive at the truth. In a later essay (*Why I Took to Philosophy*, 1955), Russell explains the difference by describing two kinds of philosophers. There are those like Bradley who believe that the world is a **whole**, like a bowl of jelly, and that to envisage it as made up of differences and individual components is both misguided and wrong.

OTHER PHILOSOPHERS ARE "ATOMISTIC" AND THINK THAT THE ONLY WAY TO CONCEIVE OF AND UNDERSTAND THE UNIVERSE IS TO REDUCE EVERYTHING TO THE **SMALLEST UNITS** POSSIBLE...

Democritus
the Atomist
460-370 B.C.

FOR THEM, AS FOR ME, THE WORLD IS MORE LIKE A "BUCKET OF SHOT".

19

G.E. Moore and Propositions

G.E. Moore's essay *The Nature of Judgement* (1899) helped to bury Idealist philosophy. Moore said that there was one central flaw with Idealism. Idealists are so called because they insist that only ideas are "real" in a world of misleading "appearances". Moore was a "realist". He replied that it is crucial to distinguish between **propositions** and our **belief** in them. (Propositions are usually sentences that "propose" or assert something: "The cat is black.")

THE CAT IS BLACK

PROPOSITIONS HAVE AN EXISTENCE OF THEIR OWN, QUITE SEPARATE FROM OUR BELIEF IN THEM. THEY ARE MUCH MORE THAN MERE IDEAS IN THE HUMAN MIND.

*FURTHERMORE, THEY ARE COMPLEX – THEY NEED TO BE **ANALYSED**, BROKEN DOWN INTO SMALLER "CONCEPTS", IF THEY ARE TO BE FULLY UNDERSTOOD.*

For Russell, this sort of analysis would become a kind of metaphysical activity – an indirect way of dissecting the world so that it could be understood.

The Foundations of Mathematics

Russell's main interest was in the foundations of mathematics. Like all knowledge, mathematics has to start from somewhere and needs rules in order to function.

$$\sqrt[3]{8} = 2$$

No argument can ever be self-justifying. Empiricist philosophers like Russell spent a lot of time trying to show that all philosophical argument and ideas can be traced back to direct experience. But no one "experiences" mathematics in the world – numbers aren't like trees or patches of colour.

So what is mathematics based on?

What is Mathematics?

Russell was convinced that mathematics had to be a perfect system of guaranteed truths about the world, and that it had a real "Platonic" existence – numbers were "real" and not just a matter of human convenience. But more importantly, he was convinced that there were some profound objective truths which ultimately constituted the whole extraordinary edifice of mathematics.

He became increasingly convinced that these fundamental ideas were to be found not in some airy "intuition", but in **Logic**.

Principles of Mathematics (1903), Russell's first great work on the foundations of mathematics, demonstrates how mathematics and logic are similar in many respects. Both are concerned with the complicated relationship between wholes and parts; to understand something actually means "to break it down into parts". Great mathematicians like **Georg Cantor** (1845-1918) showed Russell that complex notions like continuity, infinity, space and time, and matter and motion can be better conceived of as relations between numbers.

I ALSO MET THE ITALIAN **GIUSEPPE PEANO** (1858-1932) WHO INSISTED THAT THE WHOLE OF ARITHMETIC COULD BE BASED ON THREE BASIC IDEAS...

THOSE OF "ZERO", "NUMBER" AND "SUCCESSOR".

... AND FIVE FUNDAMENTAL AXIOMS.

23

The Breakthrough

Russell became convinced that mathematics is essentially based on logic in some way – a belief that his ex-teacher, **A.N. Whitehead** (1861-1947), shared.

But in order to pursue this "logicist" quest, Russell had to invent a whole new kind of "symbolic logic" and define mathematical notions in terms of this logic, both of which he proceeded to do. That is probably why he is still one of the most important philosophers of the 20th century.

The Logic of Classes

What Russell had to do was redefine mathematical notions in terms of logical ones and show how the axioms of mathematics can be derived from a logical system. He quickly saw that the relation of the whole to its parts was similar, if not identical, to the relation of a class to its members. Classes are also more flexible. The class of "ducks" can exist without having to conceive of all ducks as some unwieldy "whole".

THIS CLASS IS REALLY JUST A LOGICAL CONCLUSION ENTAILED BY THE CONCEPT OF "DUCK" AND SEEMS TO BE LOGICALLY PRIOR TO THE CONCEPT OF "NUMBER".

SO IF THE NOTION OF "CLASS" CAN BE USED TO DEFINE NUMBERS, THEN ALL OF MATHEMATICS CAN BE BUILT ON SOME KIND OF THEORY ABOUT CLASSES.

The Eureka Moment

Russell was now certain that he had solved the enigma of mathematics.

AT LAST HE KNEW WHAT MATHEMATICS WAS AND BELIEVED HE COULD SHOW THAT IT HAD SOLID FOUNDATIONS...

IT WAS LIKE CLIMBING A MOUNTAIN IN A MIST, WHEN, ON REACHING THE SUMMIT, THE MIST SUDDENLY CLEARS.

UNFORTUNATELY, I HAD ALREADY COME TO THE SAME CONCLUSION.

The German philosopher **Gottlob Frege** (1848-1925) had done much of the hard work necessary to prove it. So Russell spent many years' hard work duplicating something that had already been done.

Mathematics as an Escape

Russell didn't spend every single moment of his life doing mathematics – although he later said that it felt that way at the time. He was also interested in politics and social problems. He had met many famous socialist "Fabians" like Sidney and Beatrice Webb, George Bernard Shaw and H.G. Wells.

I CAME TO THINK THAT ENGLISH SOCIETY WAS DEEPLY UNJUST.

WE ALL FOUND HIM ASTONISHINGLY CLEVER AND AMUSING, BUT NOT ALWAYS VERY SYMPATHETIC OR TACTFUL.

ONE REASON FOR THIS REMOTENESS WAS HIS INCREASINGLY UNHAPPY MARRIAGE.

SO MATHEMATICS BECAME A KIND OF ESCAPE.

"The world of mathematics… is really a beautiful world; it has nothing to do with life and death and human sordidness, but is eternal; cold and passionless… mathematics is the only thing we know that is capable of perfection."

27

Russell's Devastating Paradox

Russell felt he had proved that mathematics had certain and unshakeable foundations in logic, established by his theory of classes. But then something puzzling and devastating occurred to him. Fairly obviously, most classes aren't members of themselves – the class of cats isn't itself a cat. So, it is possible to conceive of a rather large, if odd class: the class of all classes that are (like the cat one) not members of themselves. But then something odd happens: If the class of all classes that are not members of themselves is a member of itself, then it isn't; and if it isn't, then it is.

LET'S IMAGINE A CATALOGUE OF ALL CATALOGUES. IS IT, OR IS IT NOT, A MEMBER OF ITSELF?

– if the catalogue "of all catalogues" includes itself as a member, then it is simply **one more** catalogue among **all** catalogues and is therefore **not** a catalogue of all catalogues.

– OR, to put the same idea in another way –

– it is simply one more **class** of catalogue among all other classes of catalogues...

– if this (or any) class of all classes **is** a member of itself – as a catalogue of all catalogues **is** a catalogue – then it should not be in this class which is reserved for those which are not members of themselves...

– however, if it **is not** a member of itself – as indeed a class of all classes cannot be a class of itself – as, e.g., a "group of men" is not a man – then it should be in this class and is therefore a member of itself.

Which is Russell's point: any set "X" (e.g., a catalogue of all catalogues) is a member of itself if, and only if, it is not a member of itself. This is self-contradictory.

On the surface, Russell's paradox seems a mere verbal game, like the Cretan Liar one.

THE CRETAN PHILOSOPHER EPIMENIDES FAMOUSLY SAID...

"ALL CRETANS ARE LIARS."

SO IF HE'S TELLING THE TRUTH ABOUT ALL CRETANS, THEN HE'S LYING...

BUT IF HE'S LYING, HE'S TELLING THE TRUTH...

Russell's class paradox seems to indicate that there is something fundamentally unstable about the notion of classes, which makes it unsuitable as a totally reliable foundation for all of mathematics. Russell tried desperately to avoid this paradox (or "antinomy") with a new theory of different logical "types", and thus dispense with class theory altogether.

29

A Sense of Disillusionment

Russell never felt quite the same inspirational joy after this discovery. It undermined his conviction that mathematical knowledge could be made certain in the way that he had hoped.

"I WANTED CERTAINTY IN THE KIND OF WAY IN WHICH PEOPLE WANT RELIGIOUS FAITH... HAVING CONSTRUCTED AN ELEPHANT ON WHICH THE MATHEMATICAL WORLD COULD REST, I FOUND THE ELEPHANT TOTTERING AND PROCEEDED TO CONSTRUCT A TORTOISE TO KEEP THE ELEPHANT FROM FALLING. BUT THE TORTOISE WAS NO MORE SECURE THAN THE ELEPHANT, AND AFTER SOME 20 YEARS OF VERY ARDUOUS TOIL, I CAME TO THE CONCLUSION THAT THERE WAS NOTHING MORE THAT I COULD DO IN THE WAY OF MAKING MATHEMATICAL KNOWLEDGE INDUBITABLE."

Russell then found out that Frege had already been constructing his own monumental work (*Basic Laws of Arithmetic*, 1893-1903) which took up a very similar "logicist" position about mathematical truths. Russell wrote to him in 1902 and informed him about the "class" paradox.

I RECEIVED ONE OF THE MOST FAMOUS REPLIES IN THE HISTORY OF MATHEMATICAL PHILOSOPHY...

"YOUR DISCOVERY OF THE CONTRADICTION HAS SURPRISED ME BEYOND WORDS, AND I SHOULD LIKE TO SAY, LEFT ME THUNDERSTRUCK BECAUSE IT HAS ROCKED THE GROUND ON WHICH I MEANT TO BUILD ARITHMETIC... I MUST GIVE SOME FURTHER THOUGHT TO THE MATTER."

Principia Mathematica

Nevertheless, this puzzle did not stop Russell embarking, with Whitehead, on his most famous work, *Principia Mathematica* (named after Sir Isaac Newton's *Philosophiae Naturalis Principia Mathematica*, or "The Mathematical Principles of Natural Philosophy", 1687). Russell's aim was to demonstrate how the whole of mathematics could be reduced to logical terms. It was a mammoth task. Russell estimated that it took him 9 years to write, working on average 10 to 12 hours a day. It was published in 1910-13, and both authors had to pay part of the publication costs.

Russell had to construct layers of theory upon theory in order to prove that mathematics had its basis in logic. He also had to invent a new kind of logic – one without classes. At first he hoped to rely on what he called "substitute theory", but then realized this could give rise to more paradoxes of the "vicious circle" variety.

SO, FINALLY I INSISTED THAT THERE ARE NO SUCH THINGS AS PROPOSITIONS OUT IN THE WORLD – "SUBSISTING" IN SOME PECULIAR WAY. THERE ARE ONLY SYMBOLS THAT NEED TO BE IN SOMEONE'S MIND AND THEN JUDGED AS TRUE OR FALSE.

Types, Functions and Levels

Russell had to find a solution to his worrying "class of all classes" paradox. So he introduced a hierarchy of **types of things** that limits what can be sensibly said. For instance, I can say "Socrates is a famous philosopher" but not "A group of Athenians is a famous philosopher". Although this might seem obvious, it limits or offsets the paradox implicit in saying "a catalogue of all catalogues is a catalogue".

TYPES OF THINGS

SOCRATES ↓ **X**

FUNCTIONS

And this is a step crucial to dissolving the problem of "classes" by means of a theory of propositional **functions** – also known as "open sentences". For instance, the "Socrates" in the sentence "Socrates is wise" can be replaced by a variable "X", so as to produce the open sentence "X is wise". An open sentence can be turned into a genuine sentence by replacing the variable "X" with a quantifying expression...

X ↓ **SOCRATES**

There is an X such that X is wise

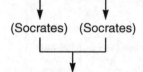

    (Socrates)   (Socrates)

       (Someone) is wise   }   a well-formed sentence

Russell's view is that profound discoveries can be made about the world from the **correct logical form** that mirrors it. There are two consequences to this. First, to expose ill-formed statements as meaningless; and second, that logically correct propositions must abandon everyday expressions. To achieve these aims, Russell proposed **levels of elements** in his theory of types…

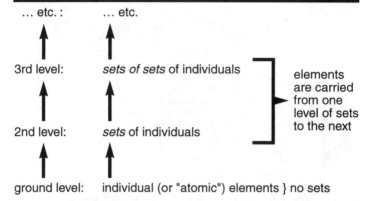

… etc. : … etc.

3rd level: *sets of sets* of individuals ⎤
2nd level: *sets* of individuals ⎬ elements are carried from one level of sets to the next
ground level: individual (or "atomic") elements } no sets ⎦

This hierarchy is intended:

▶ **1.** to show that "infinity" is reducible to its (sets of) elements
▶ **2.** to rule out –
  (a) a "set of all sets" and
  (b) a set which has itself as a member

Any statement which contradicts one or other of these rules is "ill-formed" and meaningless.

How Certain is Certainty?

What's happened? Russell has reduced mathematics to statements about classes – which are themselves dissolved in a theory of propositional functions – which also disappear into a theory of different levels to avoid circularity and paradox in judgements of true or false. But is the outcome **certain**? *Principia Mathematica* is an outrageously complicated logic which relies on some ad hoc axioms that cannot be proven and might be wrong.

In 1931, KURT GÖDEL (1906-78) came along with his "Incompleteness Theorem" which showed that my great quest was inherently impossible.

What my Incompleteness Theorem says is that, no matter how hard anyone tries, no one will ever be able to reduce all of mathematics to the application of fixed rules - including those of logic.

PRINCIPIA MATHEMATICA ?

Gödel's Incompleteness Theorem

As we have seen, mathematics "works" by building up logically valid arguments derived from a few fundamental axioms that seem so basic and self-evident that they just have to be true. And you then prove whether something is true or false by seeing whether you can prove it from your original axioms. If you can't, then you assume you've overlooked an important one and add it to your list. (This was very much Russell's procedure.)

What Gödel's theorem states is that you will never be able to find enough axioms, no matter how many you keep adding…

*THERE WILL ALWAYS BE SOME QUESTIONS YOU CANNOT **COMPLETELY** ANSWER.*

ONE SERIOUS QUESTION YOU CANNOT ANSWER IS WHETHER YOUR GROUP OF AXIOMS IS CONSISTENT OR NOT.

SO MATHEMATICS WAS NEVER A PERFECT SYSTEM OF ETERNAL TRUTHS AND NEVER COULD BE.

For Russell, this was an absolute disaster which changed his whole life. He desperately wanted something to be perfect that never could be.

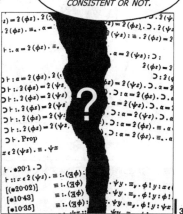

37

Conclusions Thus Far

But even if Russell and Whitehead never achieved their final and unreachable goal, they did achieve a great deal. They showed that a huge amount (if not all) of mathematics can be derived from logic. They revolutionized logic utterly. Before *Principia Mathematica*, logic hadn't developed far from relatively simple Aristotelian deduction.

ALL DOGS HAVE HEADS. THIS IS A DOG...

...THEREFORE IT HAS A HEAD.

Russell helped to show that traditional logic was only a very small part of a much bigger system. But the personal cost was high. He felt that the 9 years he devoted to the book had damaged him psychologically.

WRITING THOSE THREE VOLUMES WORE ME OUT, AND I NEVER REALLY FULLY RECOVERED FROM ALL THAT WORK.

"I FELT MORE OR LESS AS PEOPLE FEEL AT THE DEATH OF AN ILL-TEMPERED INVALID WHOM THEY HAVE NURSED AND HATED FOR YEARS."

The Strange World of Logic

Russell was one of the founders of modern symbolic logic. In order to show that mathematics was ultimately logical, he had to invent a whole new kind of "mathematical logic". (Some philosophers would now say that instead of logicizing mathematics, Russell actually mathematicized logic.) The process of symbolizing logic was well underway by the time Russell started his major work. Using symbols for logical concepts and arguments – rather like algebra – encouraged the notion that ordinary language was a wholly inadequate tool for the purposes of thought. In the late 19th century, mathematical logicians such as Frege, Peano, Cantor and the American **C.S. Peirce** (1839-1914) had devised new kinds of logic to examine the true nature of mathematics.

THE USE OF SYMBOLS ALSO ADVANCED THE IDEA THAT IT MIGHT BE POSSIBLE TO ACCELERATE AND IMPROVE HUMAN THOUGHT PROCESSES...

... OR EVEN REPLACE THEM WITH MECHANICAL OR ELECTRONIC DEVICES (LIKE THE ONE I AM USING TO WRITE THIS BOOK).

Analytic Questions of Logic

In order to invent a new kind of logic, Russell had to analyse how the deep structures of thought (and argument) relate to each other, to objects and events in the world. This is where his philosophy gets very technical. But the questions he tried to answer seem simple enough.

▶ WHAT DOES IT MEAN TO BE RATIONAL? IS IT SOMETHING THAT CAN BE DEFINED?

▶ WHAT IS THE RELATIONSHIP OF LOGIC TO TRUTH? CAN LOGIC PROVE SOMETHING TO BE TRUE, AND IF SO, HOW?

▶ WHAT ARE THE AXIOMS AND RULES OF LOGIC? HOW AND WHY ARE THEY JUSTIFIED?

▶ WHAT SORT OF LINGUISTIC STRUCTURES DOES LOGIC WORK WITH? WORDS? SENTENCES? PROPOSITIONS? JUDGEMENTS?

▶ HOW ARE COMPLEX PROPOSITIONS TO BE ANALYSED AND DECONSTRUCTED? IF YOU DO THIS, HOW DO YOU KNOW WHERE TO STOP? WHAT ARE THESE MOST BASIC ELEMENTS OR "SIMPLE PROPOSITIONS" — AND WHAT SORT OF RELATIONS DO OR SHOULD THEY HAVE BETWEEN EACH OTHER?

▶ WHAT IS THE RELATIONSHIP BETWEEN NAMES AND THE THINGS THEY REFER TO? (RUSSELL THOUGHT THAT NAMES WERE REALLY AN ENCODED KIND OF DESCRIPTION UNIQUE TO THE NAMED OBJECT.)

▶ WHAT DO PREDICATES REFER TO? UNIVERSALS? CONCEPTS? CLASSES? FOR INSTANCE, THE PREDICATE IN THE SECOND HALF OF THE PROPOSITION "RUSSELL'S HAIR IS WHITE."

WHAT IS ITS FUNCTION?

DOES IT STAND FOR SOME MYSTERIOUS **UNIVERSAL** PROPERTY OF "WHITENESS", EXPRESS OUR **CONCEPT** OF "WHITENESS" OR DOES IT REFER TO THE **CLASS** OF ALL WHITE THINGS IN SOME WAY?

41

What is Logic?

One fundamental "law" of logic states: "Nothing can be both A and not-A" (i.e., nothing can be simultaneously both a duck and not a duck). Most philosophers before Russell thought that this kind of law was fundamental because it was a direct result of how the human mind works – it's so blindingly obvious when we think about it. So logic was an aspect of human *psychology* – that which is unambiguously clear in our minds. Other philosophers besides Russell disagreed.

LOGIC HAS LITTLE TO DO WITH THE LIMITATIONS OF THE HUMAN MIND BUT IS MORE LIKE A MIRROR OF HOW THE UNIVERSE WORKS.

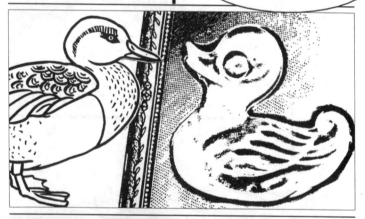

THE LOGICAL RULE ABOUT DUCKS REFLECTS THE FACT THAT REAL DUCKS IN THE WORLD CANNOT BE BOTH DUCKS AND NOT-DUCKS AT THE SAME TIME.

This means that a study of the structure of logic is also a study of the possible deep structures of reality itself. This is why Russell took logic so seriously.

Unfortunately, most (but not all) modern philosophers now disagree. For them, logic has nothing to do with the human mind and is not a mirror of the way things are. It is merely "analytic" (see page 17) – it demonstrates how one can "unpack" the implications that automatically follow when we assign meanings to certain concepts and relational terms.

SO, ALL WE LEARN FROM THE DUCK RULE IS HOW WORDS LIKE "NOTHING", "BE", "SIMULTANEOUSLY", "BOTH", "AND" AND "NOT" CAN PRODUCE CERTAIN INEVITABLE CONCLUSIONS.

Logic has little to do with the limitations of the human mind but is more like a mirror of how the universe works.

LOGIC, IN OTHER WORDS, IS AN EMPTY PROCESS OF LINGUISTIC ANALYSIS.

This was a view that Russell himself seems finally to have acknowledged but which he still found deeply distressing.

Lady Ottoline Morell

By 1909, Russell's first marriage was over in all but name. In this year, he met **Lady Ottoline Morell**, a major influence on his life. He had a complicated and unsatisfactory affair with her that lasted many years. They remained friends until she died in 1938. He wrote thousands of letters to her in which he confessed to deep feelings of loneliness and alienation, and she refers to him constantly in her journals.

Lady Ottoline was having affairs with several other men, and still loved her husband, the Liberal Member of Parliament Phillip Morell. She introduced Russell to writers and intellectuals – **Joseph Conrad** (1857-1924), **D.H. Lawrence** (1885-1930), **Lytton Strachey** (1880-1932) and **Maynard Keynes** (1883-1946). They also collaborated on a rather bad "novel of ideas", *The Perplexities of John Forstice* (1912), in which a fictionalized Russell encounters various characters with different views on philosophy, relationships and religion. Lady Ottoline came to tire of Russell's character and behaviour towards her.

I INCREASINGLY FELT THAT I WANTED CHILDREN - SOMETHING THAT LADY OTTOLINE COULD NOT PROVIDE.

HE IS LIKE A DELICATE FINE ELECTRIC INSTRUMENT, BUT NOT FED BY ORDINARY LIFE, ONLY BY THEORIES... HE HAS ONLY INTELLECTUAL UNDERSTANDING.

Empiricism and British Empiricists

Russell was an empiricist philosopher like many other great British philosophers before him. Empiricism maintains that most, or even all, of human knowledge is derived from our experience of the world.

The most obvious problem is that our experience of the world seems to be **indirect**.

Most empiricist philosophers are "**representative**" and "**causal realists**" who maintain that what we actually experience is a **representation** or copy of the world in our minds **caused** by material objects "out there".

THE PROBLEM IS THAT WE HAVE NO WAY OF KNOWING WHETHER OUR PERSONAL "COPY" IS AN ACCURATE ONE OF WHAT IS "OUT THERE".

WE KNOW THAT SOMETIMES OUR SENSES MISLEAD US - SUCH AS WHEN WE SEE A "BENT" STICK IN WATER.

SO HOW DO WE KNOW THAT OUR SENSES AREN'T MISLEADING US ALL THE TIME?

The problem is as old as philosophy itself but one that especially worried British philosophers like **John Locke** (1632-1704), **George Berkeley** (1685-1753), **David Hume** (1711-76), John Stuart Mill and Russell himself.

Descartes, Locke and Empirical Truth

The French philosopher **René Descartes** (1596-1650) insisted that
empirical knowledge could never have the kind of guaranteed certainty of
mathematics and logic. All we can ever be certain of is that we are **thinking**
and so existing in some way.

Because God is benevolent, then our sensory experiences of the world are
probably roughly accurate, but can never be certain. John Locke agreed
that there was no guarantee that our senses told us the truth about colour,
smell or taste.

These sense "qualities" exist only in us and not in objects themselves. Objects have the "power" to create these apparently empirical qualities in our minds.

It's a question that automatically arises if you envisage a thing as a "substance" which somehow irradiates "qualities" to the human mind. Locke concluded that "matter" just had to exist in some way, even though its reality inevitably remains hidden from us.

Berkeley, the Idealist Sceptic

An Idealist maintains that **only ideas** exist. George Berkeley employed persuasive arguments to suggest that only our private sensory experiences actually exist – there is no mysterious "matter" underlying them.

THE WORLD OF OBJECTS OUTSIDE US DOES NOT EXIST. ALL WE EVER PERCEIVE ARE CONSISTENT "BUNDLES" OF QUALITIES.

SO AN "APPLE" **IS** A BUNDLE OF COLOUR, SHAPE, SMELL AND TASTE - A KIND OF "APPLE EXPERIENCE".

Our illusion of these experiences stays consistent and reliable because they all exist in the mind of God.

Human beings inevitably, but wrongly, believe that their experiences emanate from an independent world "out there" that doesn't exist. It's a weird theory, but one that is very difficult for philosophers to disprove.

IF YOU ACCEPT BERKELEY'S ARGUMENTS, YOU ALSO HAVE TO ACCEPT THAT UNPERCEIVED OBJECTS (IN THE ROOM NEXT DOOR) DO NOT EXIST...

*TO BE IS TO BE **PERCEIVED.***

Unperceived objects only "exist" as potential experiences waiting for you – conveniently stored in the mind of God. The agnostic Russell's epistemology (theory of knowledge) and ontology (what is or isn't real) is very like Berkeley's.

Hume on Impressions

David Hume agreed with Berkeley, but said that it was impossible for human beings to live like that. We may be able to accept sceptical arguments that show us that our experiences of the world are **dubitable** (they can be doubted), but these will never have any real effect on our everyday lives. Hume then goes on to demolish many other philosophical "certainties" by examining them with a sceptical and empiricist approach. Human beings are exceedingly inventive – they habitually produce all kinds of ideas – about God, for example.

In the end, Hume says, there is very little of our knowledge that we **can** prove, outside of mathematics and logic.

Mill's Phenomenalism

Russell's godfather, John Stuart Mill, stayed within this tradition. His philosophy of perception doesn't take things much further. His version of empiricism is often known as "Phenomenalism" – only phenomena that we experience exist.

WE CAN TRY TO SOLVE THE SCEPTICS' PROBLEM OF "UNPERCEIVED OBJECTS" BY CLAIMING THAT THEY ARE "PERMANENT POSSIBILITIES OF SENSATION"...

WHICH DOESN'T MAKE THE PROBLEM MUCH CLEARER OR BRING IT CLOSER TO ANY SORT OF SOLUTION.

Russell's Theory of Knowledge

One of the most famous works by Russell is entitled *Lectures on the Philosophy of Logical Atomism*, first published in 1918. Although Russell's philosophy continually evolved and was never a monolithic doctrine, this label stuck. "Logical Atomism" is more traditional and less scientific than it actually sounds.

"ATOMISM" MEANS THAT YOU BREAK THINGS DOWN INTO THEIR SMALLEST COMPONENTS, IF YOU WANT TO UNDERSTAND THEM.

"LOGICAL" MEANS THAT YOU REASSEMBLE THEM LOGICALLY, RATHER THAN BY USING GUESSWORK, IF YOU WANT TO BE CERTAIN OF WHAT YOU ARE THINKING ABOUT.

Russell makes the old philosophical problem of perception sound technical and scientific by referring to "sense-data" rather than "ideas" or "impressions" – but his empiricism isn't greatly different from Hume's.

Russell agrees that all we can ever experience are appearances. That which we **directly** experience he calls "sense-data" and that which **awaits** our experience, "sensibilia".

SO, FOR ME, MOUNT EVEREST IS, AND PROBABLY ALWAYS WILL BE, A CLUSTER OF SENSIBILIA...

... WHEREAS THE PATCHES OF SHAPE AND COLOUR THAT SURROUND ME IN THIS ROOM ARE THE IMMEDIATE SENSE-DATA WITH WHICH I AM NOW, AT THIS VERY MOMENT, ACQUAINTED.

Our experience of the world can be broken down into the thousands of such bits or "atoms" experienced only fleetingly and privately, and which cannot usually be named except with words like "this". Sense-data exist only as long as the person experiencing them. But at least they are indubitable, unlike physical objects themselves, which are merely inferences.

A Logical Hypothesis

So the real world is only a hypothesis. And the more one disassembles experience, the closer one will get to the truth. I can, if I like, infer from these clusters of data that I am sitting in a room, in front of a computer screen, but I cannot guarantee that this is the case.

ALL I CAN BE ABSOLUTELY CERTAIN OF IS THE EXISTENCE OF THESE FLEETING AND PRIVATE SENSE-DATA.

AND THE SENSE-DATA THEMSELVES ARE NEITHER WHOLLY **MENTAL** NOR WHOLLY **PHYSICAL** ENTITIES, BUT SOMETHING STRANGELY BETWEEN THE TWO.

But Logical Atomism is more than just a theory of perception. It is also a theory about meaning and metaphysics. And to see why this is, we have to understand Russell's most famous essay, *On Denoting*.

On Denoting

This short essay, written in 1905, is probably Russell's most famous and influential. Every student of philosophy ends up studying it sooner or later. It is a work of pure academic philosophy and not an easy read, so take it slowly...

Most of us would agree that the two most obvious functions of language are, first of all, to **refer** to things, and then to **describe** them.

ROME   IS SUNNY.

(REFERRING)   (DESCRIBING)

FATHER   IS GOING.

REFERRING (OR DENOTING) IS HOW MOST OF US LEARN LANGUAGE IN THE FIRST PLACE – BY ASSOCIATING CERTAIN NOISES AND MARKS ON PAPER WITH OBJECTS OR PICTURES OF OBJECTS.

SAY "DUCK"! LOOK AT THE DUCK!

We might instinctively agree that referring is an obvious fact about how we use words, and maybe even how words get their meaning. That's clear. Or is it?

Language and Reality

Referring is also how words relate to the world. Any theory about how words refer will almost automatically include a theory about what exists "out there" for language to refer to.

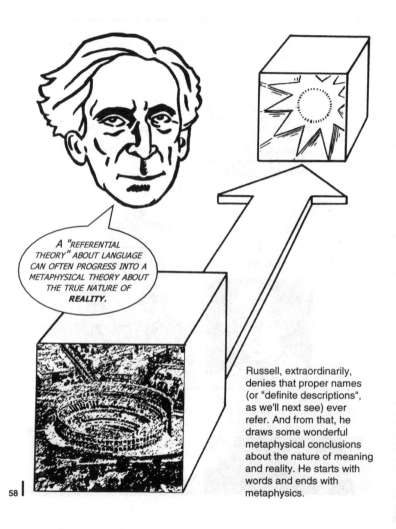

A "REFERENTIAL THEORY" ABOUT LANGUAGE CAN OFTEN PROGRESS INTO A METAPHYSICAL THEORY ABOUT THE TRUE NATURE OF **REALITY**.

Russell, extraordinarily, denies that proper names (or "definite descriptions", as we'll next see) ever refer. And from that, he draws some wonderful metaphysical conclusions about the nature of meaning and reality. He starts with words and ends with metaphysics.

Definite Descriptions

Expressions that refer (all of them called confusingly "proper names"
by Russell) are those like: "Wendy Smith", "Paris", **as well as** "she", "the
present President of America", and so on. But referring expressions can
produce weird paradoxes, especially if you believe, as Russell did, in a
referential theory of meaning – that is, words get their meaning **by** referring.
In his essay, Russell's focus is mainly on "definite descriptions" – phrases
that begin with the definite article "the" – as in "the present Queen of
England", "the man in the sentry box".

WE CAN ALL SEE
THAT AN EXPRESSION LIKE
"THE AVERAGE MAN" - AS IN
"THE AVERAGE MAN DRINKS SIX PINTS
OF BEER A WEEK" - CLEARLY DOES
NOT REFER TO ONE
PERSON.

RATHER,
IT IS AN ECONOMICAL
(IF POTENTIALLY CONFUSING)
WAY OF TALKING ABOUT **ALL MEN**
AND THEIR DRINKING
HABITS.

NOT MANY
PEOPLE WOULD THINK
OF "THE AVERAGE MAN"
AS A REFERRING
EXPRESSION.

Paradoxes and Puzzles

But, if you say that "The first man to fly unaided does not exist", then who are you referring to? It can't be "the first man" (because he doesn't exist – remember!). So what is "the first man"? Some kind of nonsense? If so, then the whole sentence must be gibberish. But it doesn't sound like gibberish. Russell's most famous example of this kind of puzzle is his sentence, **"The present King of France is bald"** – a good example of the sort of paradox that referring expressions can cause.

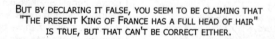

THIS SENTENCE SEEMS TO BE FALSE – THERE IS NO KING OF FRANCE.

BUT BY DECLARING IT FALSE, YOU SEEM TO BE CLAIMING THAT "THE PRESENT KING OF FRANCE HAS A FULL HEAD OF HAIR" IS TRUE, BUT THAT CAN'T BE CORRECT EITHER.

Logicians like propositions (sentences that assert something) to be either true or false, and this paradoxical assertion about the French King seems, strangely, to be neither. Nor does it appear to be nonsense.

More worrying still is the fact that a referring expression like **"The Home Secretary has a full head of hair"** means something at the moment, and yet it would **still** mean something if he had died during the night. The meaning remains the same, whether there is a living Home Secretary or not.

"THE HOME SECRETARY" CANNOT BE A REFERRING EXPRESSION WHEN THERE IS **NO SUCH PERSON**, BUT NEITHER IS IT, IF THERE **IS**, BECAUSE THE EXPRESSION MEANS THE SAME IN EITHER CASE.

*MEANING COMES FROM **REFERRING**, REMEMBER?*

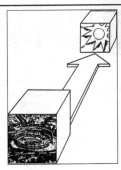

Other paradoxes also arise, like those to do with identity (as in "Scott is the author of *Waverley*" where Russell insists that neither can ultimately be referring expressions). So, if we insist on keeping referring expressions like "the so-and-so", then we end up asserting that sentences like "The so-and-so does not exist" can never be true and that some propositions are, weirdly, neither true nor false, nor nonsense.

Russell's Solution

Russell's solution to these paradoxes is his famous "Theory of Descriptions". What Russell does is to show that these apparently simple sentences in ordinary everyday language are really much more complex when you analyse them **logically**.

So "**THE** PRESENT KING OF FRANCE IS BALD" BECOMES...

THERE EXISTS ONE AND ONLY ONE ENTITY WHICH IS **A** KING OF FRANCE, AND WHICH IS BALD.

WHAT THE ANALYSIS REVEALS OF COURSE IS THE HIDDEN **EXISTENCE** CLAIM CONTAINED IN THE WORD "THE" - REPLACED BY THE INDEFINITE "A".

Russell claims that this is true of all referring expressions which take this form.

"**THE** A IS B" REALLY MEANS "THERE EXISTS ONE AND ONLY ONE ENTITY WHICH IS **AN** A, AND WHICH IS B".

The Conclusion About Words and Referring

Russell's conclusion from this logical analysis of puzzling expressions is his claim that all proper names are **disguised descriptions**. So "The King of France" gets demoted to "One entity that has the **property** of being a French King" (and the property of baldness, of course). The new and more logical "There exists one and only one entity which has the property of being a French King" is much less puzzling and now clearly revealed as false.

"THE CAT IS A CARNIVORE" MEANS "IF ANYTHING HAS THE PROPERTY OF BEING A CAT, THEN IT HAS THE PROPERTY OF BEING A CARNIVORE."

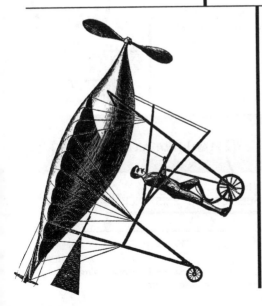

AND THAT PUZZLING SENTENCE ABOUT THE NON-EXISTENT "FLYING MAN" BECOMES "THERE DOES NOT EXIST ONE AND ONLY ONE ENTITY WHICH IS A MAN AND WHICH CAN FLY UNAIDED."

63

Grammatical Existence

Logical analysis of Russell's kind shows how confusing ordinary language can be, how it can lead to odd paradoxes, and how the only way to solve them is to analyse ordinary language into its clearer "logical form".

WHEN YOU DO THIS, YOU FIND THAT **GRAMMATICAL** SUBJECTS ARE USUALLY NOT **LOGICAL** ONES.

PUZZLING PROBLEMS ABOUT MYSTERIOUS "EMPTY" DENOTING PHRASES ("**THE** KING OF FRANCE") ARE SOLVED.

AND MANY PARADOXES - LIKE THE ONE ABOUT "THE CLASS OF CLASSES THAT ARE NOT MEMBERS OF THEMSELVES" - ARE SHOWN TO BE ILLUSORY.

The confusions that arise when "existence" is regarded as a "property" of things disappears. Logic no longer has to be based on the Subject-Predicate Form.

ANALYSE THIS:

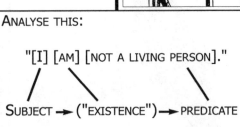

"[I] [AM] [NOT A LIVING PERSON]."

SUBJECT ➝ ("EXISTENCE") ➝ PREDICATE

Newer and more complex relations between propositions are made possible and a new kind of predicate logic is born.

Logical Atomism as a System

The easiest way to understand Russell's philosophy is to imagine him constantly and ruthlessly chucking away all the knowledge he thinks is at all dubitable, and seeing what we're left with. He also makes the assumption that the best way to get at the truth is to reduce everything to its simplest components. What we're finally left with, he thinks, is very small bits of information about very small private sensory experiences. These "bits" he calls "logical atoms".

LOGICAL ATOMS ARE THE SMALLEST AND FINALLY IRREDUCIBLE ELEMENTS WHICH CANNOT BE ANALYSED ANY FURTHER – TO WHICH EVERYTHING IS FINALLY REDUCIBLE.

ALL TALK ABOUT OBJECTS CAN FINALLY BE REDUCIBLE TO TALK ABOUT **SENSE-DATA** – FROM WHICH WE CONSTRUCT OUR CONVENIENT "LOGICAL FICTIONS" OF MATERIAL OBJECTS.

SENSE-DATA ARE THE LOGICAL ATOMS OF THE UNIVERSE. OUR EXPERIENCE OF THEM AND REFERENCE TO THEM ARE THE ULTIMATE FOUNDATION OF MEANING. THOSE ARE THE ONLY ENTITIES OF WHICH WE CAN BE ABSOLUTELY SURE.

"THE POINT OF PHILOSOPHY IS TO START WITH SOMETHING SO SIMPLE AS NOT TO SEEM WORTH STATING, AND TO END WITH SOMETHING SO PARADOXICAL THAT NO ONE WILL BELIEVE IT."

65

What Can be Referred to?

Russell's conclusion in *On Denoting* was that most referring expressions are really coded descriptions of properties. The President of France does not need a living one for the expression to have meaning, so it must be an expression about a property (of being the President of France).

ARE THERE ANY EXPRESSIONS LEFT THAT **DO** REFER, OR ARE THEY ALL ULTIMATELY ANALYSABLE INTO DESCRIPTIONS OF PROPERTIES?

THERE ARE SOME UNIQUE ENTITIES THAT LANGUAGE HAS TO REFER TO DIRECTLY WITH EXPRESSIONS REFERRING TO IMMEDIATE AND DIRECT SENSE-DATA – WORDS LIKE "THIS" OR "THAT".

Because sense-data are private experiences of patches of colour and shapes, the only way we can talk about them is to say "this" or "that". Russell, remember, thinks that all we can ever be sure about are "sense-data", not real objects in the world.

Russell and Berkeley

So what happens to things like tables, cats and kings, and our knowledge and talk about them?

SUCH THINGS EXIST, BUT ALL WE CAN EVER KNOW ABOUT THEM IS OUR SENSORY EXPERIENCES OF THEIR PROPERTIES, EVEN IF WE CAN BE FAIRLY SURE THAT OUR EXPERIENCES OF THEIR "PRIMARY QUALITIES" ARE CORRECT.

ALL THAT WE CAN EVER EXPERIENCE ARE "QUALITIES" OR PROPERTIES. THERE IS NO REASON TO BELIEVE THERE ARE OBJECTS "OUT THERE" CAUSING OUR EXPERIENCES.

GOD CREATES THE WHOLE CONSISTENT CHARADE FOR US.

Russell's view seems closest to Berkeley's.

I AM MORE OF AN AGNOSTIC ABOUT WHETHER OR NOT THERE ARE OBJECTS "OUT THERE" CAUSING OUR EXPERIENCES OF PROPERTIES.

And he leaves God out of it.

Material objects are a bit like "the average man" – useful logical fictions but only a kind of shorthand for the complicated truth. "Material objects" is just a convenient shorthand for a complicated talk about private sense-data.

A Pure Logical Language

On Denoting is one of the most important pieces of philosophical writing in the 20th century. But not because it was a radical theory of perception or a startling piece of metaphysics. It is revolutionary because it changed the way philosophers looked at language and meaning. It encouraged philosophers to think that it might be possible to create a perfect logical language, free from all the ambiguities and confusions of "ordinary" language.

IF THIS COULD BE ACHIEVED, IT WOULD BE A POWERFUL TOOL, NOT ONLY FOR THE PURPOSE OF COMMUNICATION, BUT ALSO FOR AN INVESTIGATION OF TRADITIONAL PHILOSOPHICAL PROBLEMS.

THIS NEW POWERFUL LANGUAGE MIGHT SOLVE THESE PROBLEMS, OR AT LEAST REVEAL THEM AS INHERENTLY UNSOLVABLE.

And if it could be shown that this ideal language had a kind of one-to-one relationship with the world, it might even be a tool with which to investigate the deep possible structures of reality itself. (Russell remained convinced about that last bit. Other philosophers like Wittgenstein at first agreed but then changed their minds.)

Analytic Philosophy

On Denoting didn't only help to construct a new form of "predicate logic" but to found a whole school of philosophy now known as "analytic" or "linguistic" philosophy. The philosopher's job was to examine language and analyse what it is "really saying" when broken down into its logical components. Many 20th-century philosophers were led to think of philosophy as an analytic "activity" rather than a body of knowledge.

What mattered to Russell was whether a statement was true or false, not just what it meant. The real function of philosophy was to understand the world and the human beings that inhabit it. Russell always maintained an interest in science because it seemed to be succeeding in doing both.

Wittgenstein: Benign or Malign Influence?

Russell's Logical Atomism is a complicated theory of knowledge, meaning and metaphysics. It is a mixture of two strands – long-held empiricist beliefs about how we perceive the world, and a theory of meaning invented by **Ludwig Wittgenstein** (1889-1951) which made a deep impression on Russell. Wittgenstein's *Tractatus Logico-Philosophicus* (1922) insisted that language only has meaning because of the way it can "picture" the world. It's a strange, mystical and complex version of the "referential" theory of meaning.

ROME IS SUNNY

> *YOU ARE RIGHT THAT ORDINARY SENTENCES HAVE TO BE ANALYSED INTO COLLECTIONS OF MORE BASIC AND LOGICAL PROPOSITIONS IF THEY ARE TO BE PROPERLY UNDERSTOOD.*

For Wittgenstein, the structure of a meaningful sentence must somehow be a "mirror" or representation of the way reality is structured.

This is not Wittgenstein

When a sentence is analysed into its deepest and simplest logical form, you discover that it is made up of a series of "elementary sentences" which contain "names". These "names" then correspond to "objects" in the world. How names are arranged in these sentences must correspond to a possible arrangement of objects in the world. So names **denote** and sentences **picture**, and that's how language gets its meaning.

The Mystery of Names and Objects

Unlike Russell, Wittgenstein was reluctant to provide an example of a "name" or to say what sort of thing an "object" would be – perhaps because they are so elemental and basic. And he thought that no more could be said about how language pictures reality, because you cannot use language to delineate itself – such truths can only ever be shown.

Wittgenstein's theory of meaning is strange and wonderful, full of unexplained technical terms, and not always argued clearly.

I REJECTED MOST OF IT LATER ON IN MY LIFE. BUT IT MADE A DEEP IMPRESSION ON RUSSELL.

I TOOK IT OVER AND MADE IT INTO MY OWN THEORY OF KNOWLEDGE, MEANING AND METAPHYSICS.

Wittgenstein's mysterious "objects" become Russell's "sense-data". Russell's elementary sentences are those that refer directly to sense-data as in "This is red" (an "atomic fact"). From these elementary logical forms, the whole of meaning is constructed, and it is on these that all knowledge is ultimately derived.

But is it True?

Wittgenstein came to express grave doubts about reductive analysis as the only road to truth.

SPLITTING A BROOM INTO SMALLER AND SMALLER PIECES TELLS YOU VERY LITTLE ABOUT IT – WHAT ITS FUNCTION IS AND HOW IT IS GENERALLY USED.

Other criticisms of Logical Atomism usually focus on its theory of perception or its theory of reference and meaning. For instance...

▶ Is it true that it is sense-data that we experience, or do we actually experience the world more directly?

▶ Are sense-data the most elemental entities?

▶ Does Russell "reify" them? (Talk about them as if they were **things** rather than appearances?)

▶ Are sense-data really as indubitable and reliable as Russell thinks they are? (If they aren't, then his whole empiricist programme is in trouble.)

▶ If sense-data are **caused** by material objects, doesn't that make material objects more elemental?

▶ Does the mind passively "receive" sense-data and then construct a fictional world of things from this information, or is the mind more creative, partly creating and categorizing what it perceives in a more complicated two-way process?

▶ Can I have "private" experiences of this kind which are expressible only in some kind of "private language" of my own?

▶ Is it true to say that most referring expressions do not refer? Isn't a referring expression one that is capable of referring in certain situations, rather than one that has to all the time?

▶ Does a word or a sentence really get its meaning by referring? Or is meaning derived from something else altogether? Or is the search for what meaning is, and on what it is based, ultimately a futile quest?

Russell's Theories of Meaning

We finally come to Russell's several and different theories of meaning. Philosophers have always been interested in language and meaning, especially in the 20th century. Words and sentences are what philosophers think with, so it is crucial that language they use is clear and unambiguous. For most of his life, Russell believed that words get their meaning because they refer to things in the world.

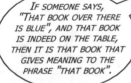

> IF SOMEONE SAYS, "THAT BOOK OVER THERE IS BLUE", AND THAT BOOK IS INDEED ON THE TABLE, THEN IT IS THAT BOOK THAT GIVES MEANING TO THE PHRASE "THAT BOOK".

THE WORDS "IS BLUE" REFER TO SOMETHING RATHER ODDER – THE ABSTRACT UNIVERSAL "BLUENESS" WITH WHICH THAT PERSON HAS ALREADY BEEN **DIRECTLY** ACQUAINTED.

This is superficially an attractive theory for many people. Pointing to things and saying a word associated with them is how most of us learn meanings. But as a **theory** of meaning it throws up many problems. One is that it encourages the idea that nouns must always stand for **something** in the world, which promotes a growth of abstract entities conjured into some kind of thin existence to prove that these words do indeed have meaning. (We've seen how Russell attempted to solve this problem in his "Theory of Descriptions".)

The Ideational or Mentalist Theory

Russell produced his own version of the more traditional empiricist account of meaning which claims that words get their meaning by referring to ideas. Words get their meaning because people use words as "marks" to convey their pre-linguistic ideas to each other. For philosophers like Locke, "ideas" are usually talked about as if they were internal mental images.

THESE "IDEATIONAL IMAGES" ARE SEEN BY THE MIND, THEN TRANSLATED INTO LANGUAGE, AND SO MOVED FROM ONE MIND INTO ANOTHER.

HENCE, LANGUAGE GETS MEANING BY REFERRING - BUT NOT TO THINGS IN THE REAL WORLD.

This theory also raises its own unique problems. It's not at all clear that all our thoughts are visual and not intrinsically verbal, and there is no guarantee that B will receive the same original "idea" as A. And how do mental pictures "mean"?

The Atomist Theory

Russell's "Atomist" theory is the final result of a radical empiricist programme which maintains that language can only have meaning if it refers, and that every individual has ultimately to be directly acquainted with that which is referred to. All that we can refer to (rather than describe) is the immediate and rapidly changing series of phenomena – "sense-data" – the most elementary sensory experiences there are. All statements about objects can and must be reduced to statements about sense-data.

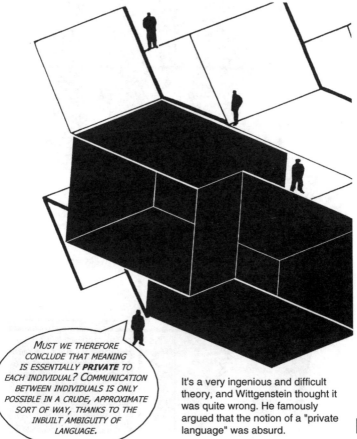

*MUST WE THEREFORE CONCLUDE THAT MEANING IS ESSENTIALLY **PRIVATE** TO EACH INDIVIDUAL? COMMUNICATION BETWEEN INDIVIDUALS IS ONLY POSSIBLE IN A CRUDE, APPROXIMATE SORT OF WAY, THANKS TO THE INBUILT AMBIGUITY OF LANGUAGE.*

It's a very ingenious and difficult theory, and Wittgenstein thought it was quite wrong. He famously argued that the notion of a "private language" was absurd.

Behavioural Theory

Later on, Russell was attracted to a different "behavioural" theory of meaning which claims that a theory of meaning must focus on the speaker's "intentions" and the "effects" these have on a listener to produce certain behavioural responses.

BUT NOT ALL WORDS DISPOSE PEOPLE TO SOME KIND OF RESPONSE...

AS A THEORY, IT RESTRICTS MEANING TO **OBSERVABLE** HUMAN BEHAVIOUR.

IT IGNORES THE FACT THAT PEOPLE CAN HAVE PRIVATE LINGUISTIC **THOUGHTS** THAT ARE NOT REVEALED BY THEIR EXTERNAL BEHAVIOUR. MEANING AND RESPONSES ARE NOT NECESSARILY THE SAME THING.

Frege's Sense and Reference

There are, of course, other theories of meaning competing with Russell's own. For instance, he knew of Frege's claim that meaning had two elements – **sense** and **reference**. Sense is a public phenomenon based on conventional agreement. We can all agree to use the sign "duck" to signify a certain kind of bird.

It was advice that Russell seems to have ignored, and partly explains why his philosophy of language seems at times to go round in circles.

Wittgenstein's "Ghost" of Meaning

Russell also knew of (and disagreed with) Wittgenstein's later view that any philosophical search for "meaning" is a mistake. The existence of the search already presupposes that "meaning" must somehow be something independent of language – like a ghost inhabiting sentences.

BUT JUST BECAUSE THE WORD "MEANING" EXISTS DOESN'T IMPLY THAT THERE IS SOME ABSTRACT ENTITY FOR IT TO REFER TO.

ALL PHILOSOPHERS CAN DO IS TO EXAMINE HOW LANGUAGE IS **USED** BY PEOPLE IN ALL SORTS OF DIFFERENT CONTEXTS.

IT IS POINTLESS LOOKING FOR MEANING IN PRIVATE INNER MENTAL PROCESSES.

Wittgenstein also later claimed that language "floats free" of the world. A study of how it is structured cannot hope to tell us anything about the fundamental configurations of the world. Philosophers can only attempt to clarify concepts and so "dissolve" many traditional philosophical "problems".

PHILOSOPHY IS OFTEN INVOLVED IN THE SEARCH FOR NON-EXISTENT ENTITIES ASSUMED TO EXIST BECAUSE OF THE BELIEF THAT WORDS HAVE A ONE-TO-ONE RELATION WITH THINGS.

TO EMPLOY A USEFUL WORD LIKE "TRUTH" DOESN'T MEAN THERE IS ONE THING THAT IT REFERS TO - AND THAT PHILOSOPHERS MUST HUNT FOR THIS MYSTERIOUS ENTITY.

PHILOSOPHY IS A BATTLE AGAINST THE BEWITCHMENT OF OUR INTELLIGENCE BY MEANS OF LANGUAGE.

The Problems of Philosophy

In 1911, Russell began writing one of his most popular books, *The Problems of Philosophy* (published in 1912). He called it his "Shilling Shocker" and never took it very seriously. It helped to make him famous and has never gone out of print. Students are still given it as a sound introduction to the subject, although nowadays it is regarded as a bit old-fashioned. In it, Russell examines many of the central problems of philosophy, primarily those of perceptual knowledge. The knowledge that we **think** we have about the world around us is one that has exercised all British "empiricist" philosophers.

I BELIEVE THAT ALL WE CAN EVER EXPERIENCE ARE THE "APPEARANCES" THAT THE WORLD PRESENTS TO US, BUT WE REMAIN IGNORANT OF ITS "REAL" NATURE.

*WE ARE TRAPPED IN THE WORLD OF THOSE SENSATIONS THAT OUR SENSORY ORGANS GIVE US AND HAVE NO REAL KNOWLEDGE OF WHAT ACTUALLY **CAUSES** THOSE SENSATIONS.*

The common-sense view is that there must be "physical objects" out there that cause us to have such sensations, but there seems no way that we can prove this is indeed the case.

Two Kinds of Knowledge

In his book, Russell also draws the famous distinction between "knowledge by acquaintance" and "knowledge by description". We are directly and immediately "acquainted" with sensations of shape and colour and we can then infer from such data that it may be physical objects that produce this data in us. Knowledge by acquaintance is indubitable, usually private, fleeting and unmediated – its origins often mysterious.

I INCLUDE MEMORIES, UNIVERSALS, AND OTHER KINDS OF SELF-CONSCIOUS THOUGHTS AND FEELINGS ALONG WITH SENSE-DATA.

KNOWLEDGE BY DESCRIPTION IS THE EASY-TO-UNDERSTAND SORT THAT ONE FINDS IN BOOKS AND OTHER INFORMATIVE SOURCES THAT CAN BE DESCRIBED AND MADE PUBLIC.

But, as we know, the logically atomistic Russell claims that nearly all knowledge by description is ultimately reducible to knowledge by acquaintance.

85

The Other Problems of Philosophy

The other problems that Russell examines are those of induction, general principles, **a priori** knowledge, universals, and truth and error. The process of induction is something that we all do, often almost instinctively. Even my cat can learn to do it.

But no one can guarantee, just because these things have been true in the past, they will be true tomorrow. Our everyday and our scientific knowledge of the universe will always be provisional and fallible, highly probable but not "guaranteed" or "necessary" in the way that the truths of maths and logic are usually thought to be.

Universals and Particulars

In the chapter on "General Principles", Russell informs his readers about the key differences between Rationalist and Empiricist philosophers. Rationalists look to cerebral necessary truths (like those of maths and logic) as the foundations for knowledge, whereas Empiricists claim that all knowledge has to begin with our experiences of the world, however puzzling and limited these may be.

*AS A CONVINCED EMPIRICIST, I STRESS THAT **A PRIORI** KNOWLEDGE - KNOWLEDGE INDEPENDENT OF EXPERIENCE - CAN TELL US NOTHING ABOUT THE WORLD, ONLY ABOUT ENTITIES WHICH DO NOT EXIST, LIKE "PROPERTIES" AND "RELATIONS".*

LET'S LOOK AT "PARTICULARS" AND "UNIVERSALS". WHAT REALITY DO SUCH UNIVERSALS HAVE - "WHITENESS", "TRIANGULARITY", "NORTH OF" (AS IN "EDINBURGH IS NORTH OF LONDON")?

Are Universals Real?

Some philosophers believe that universals are no more than convenient **words** that have no real existence, others that they are **ideas** that human beings refer to in their minds when they attempt to classify and understand the world. But like Plato, Russell believes that universals are not thoughts but "the objects of thoughts" – they are real and external to us, even if they don't exist in the way that London and Edinburgh do.

THEY HAVE A THINNER, LESS SUBSTANTIAL KIND OF EXISTENCE THAT CAN BE CALLED "BEING" OR "SUBSISTENCE"...

WHATEVER **THAT** IS! THE AGE-OLD PHILOSOPHICAL PROBLEM OF "UNIVERSALS" IS ANOTHER POINTLESS SEARCH FOR "GENERALITY". THERE ARE NO "ESSENCES" OR "UNIVERSALS" FOR "GENERAL WORDS" TO REFER TO.

What is Truth?

Russell finishes his book by examining what it is that makes our beliefs true or false. Truth has nothing to do with psychological states of mind. "What makes a belief true is a fact, and this fact does not in any way involve the mind of the person who has the belief." Philosophy, he concludes, reveals to us how little we can ever know for certain. It can tell us nothing for sure about the way things are.

SOUTH OF

WE CAN KNOW THAT THE LAW OF GRAVITATION IS HIGHLY PROBABLE - AND THAT OUR EXPERIENCE OF "SENSE-DATA" IS INDUBITABLE - BUT NOT MUCH ELSE.

Seeing as God Might See

Nevertheless, despite the uncertainty of its enterprise, philosophy is a wholly worthwhile human activity.

> *"PHILOSOPHY, THOUGH UNABLE TO TELL US WITH CERTAINTY WHAT IS THE TRUE ANSWER TO THE DOUBTS WHICH IT RAISES, IS ABLE TO SUGGEST MANY POSSIBILITIES WHICH ENLARGE OUR THOUGHTS AND FREE THEM FROM THE TYRANNY OF CUSTOM."*

> *"THE FREE INTELLECT SEES AS GOD MIGHT SEE, WITHOUT A HERE AND NOW, WITHOUT HOPES AND FEARS, WITHOUT THE TRAMMELS OF CUSTOMARY BELIEFS AND CONTEMPORARY PREJUDICES, CALMLY, DISPASSIONATELY, IN THE SOLE AND EXCLUSIVE DESIRE OF KNOWLEDGE..."*

Wittgenstein, the Prodigal Son

Although Russell was influenced by philosophers like G.E. Moore and Whitehead, the most obviously decisive thinker he ever encountered was one of his own students, Ludwig Wittgenstein. They first met in 1911.

The Ferocious Student

At first, Russell patronized his new student as "my ferocious German" but soon changed his mind when Wittgenstein began to dismiss many of the time-honoured "problems" of traditional philosophy as unimportant. He challenged Russell to think about others in a wholly new sort of way.

HE THINKS NOTHING EMPIRICAL IS KNOWABLE – I ASKED HIM TO ADMIT THAT THERE WAS NOT A RHINOCEROS IN THE ROOM, BUT HE WOULDN'T.

Russell's early relationship with Wittgenstein was extremely intense. Russell had to work hard to keep up with Wittgenstein's radical new ideas about logic, language and the world.

In some ways, Wittgenstein was like the younger Russell – he was obsessively interested in the difficult technical questions of philosophy. He felt forced to ask fundamental questions about the nature, identity and function of logic. But, unlike Russell, he never thought that philosophy should be an investigation of perceptual knowledge or "matter". Wittgenstein's philosophy centres on the problems of meaning, not knowledge.

MY AMBITION WAS TO SHOW THAT THERE WERE SEVERE LIMITS TO WHAT LANGUAGE COULD SAY - AND RUSSELL NEVER REALLY UNDERSTOOD HOW DIFFERENT THIS NEW PHILOSOPHICAL AGENDA WAS TO HIS OWN.

BUT WHAT REALLY MATTERS IS WHAT WE CAN ONLY BE SILENT ABOUT

NEVERTHELESS, FOR A SHORT TIME, I SAW WITTGENSTEIN AS MY SUCCESSOR...

I LOVE HIM AS IF HE WERE MY SON.

Parting of the Ways

Russell soon felt intimidated by Wittgenstein – not only was he too
volatile and angry, for reasons which were not always clear, but he was
also contemptuous of most of Russell's own work and his inability to
comprehend Wittgenstein's rather mystical "picture theory" of meaning.
"I could only just understand (him) by stretching my mind to the utmost."

WHEN
WITTGENSTEIN
READ MY **THEORY OF
KNOWLEDGE**, HE
DECLARED THAT "IT WAS
ALL WRONG"...

IN MY
BONES, I FELT
THAT HE MUST
BE RIGHT.

Russell became increasingly despondent about his life and achievements and confessed to Lady Ottoline that he thought he should give up philosophy for something else.

Russell assimilated some of Wittgenstein's ideas into his own philosophy with differing degrees of success. Finally, and probably inevitably, the two men quarrelled, although it is still not clear why. Wittgenstein still admired Russell, but felt that *"There cannot be any real relation of friendship between us."*

Joseph Conrad

Fortunately, not all of Russell's friends were as difficult and demanding. Lady Ottoline had introduced Russell to the Polish-born writer **Joseph Conrad** (1857-1924). Russell immediately took to him. Both men had lost their parents at an early age, both had a deep-seated fear of being struck down by insanity, and both felt isolated from the world in their belief that Western "civilization" was extremely fragile.

So impressed was Russell by the meeting that he later named two of his sons after the writer.

I DUTIFULLY READ ALL THE PHILOSOPHICAL WORKS THAT RUSSELL SENT ME...

AND I READ MOST OF CONRAD'S WORK, FINDING IN SOME OF HIS FICTIONAL CHARACTERS A PERCEPTIVE ANALYSIS OF MY OWN CONDITION.

But Russell was on the lookout for someone who could understand him. He projected a shared intimacy onto this polite relationship that was never really there as far as Conrad was concerned.

The First World War

Before 1914, Russell was well known in academic circles as a logician. By 1918, he had become a famous public and political figure. When war was declared against Germany in 1914, Russell was horrified. He spoke excellent German, was well acquainted with many German philosophers (as well as the Austrian Wittgenstein, now in Norway) and had a high regard for German culture. He was dismayed to see the fervent enthusiasm for war amongst ordinary people in the streets and thought the governments of the day played on people's instinctive but unwarranted fears of foreigners.

Russell wrote several pamphlets condemning the war. His essay *The Ethics of War* argued that war between two civilized states like Britain and Germany was madness. In January 1916, the government introduced conscription, which outraged Russell even further. By now, he was 43 and so not himself eligible for military service.

THERE IS NO MORE HORRIBLE CRIME AGAINST LIBERTY THAN TO COMPEL MEN TO KILL EACH OTHER WHEN THEIR CONSCIENCE TELLS THEM TO LIVE IN PEACE.

The Conscription Issue

Russell was a good public speaker – he talked confidently, clearly and was extremely persuasive. (He often thought that he should have pursued a career in politics rather than philosophy.) His lectures against the war were well attended and he became a leading light in the No-Conscription Fellowship which organized protests against conscription and gave support to numerous "conscientious objectors" who refused to fight. Some conscientious objectors were allowed to join the Non-Combatant Corps.

Russell was fined £100 (about £8,000 in today's terms) and threatened with imprisonment for writing in support of one objector who refused to fight **or** dig trenches.

The Pacifist Russell

By this time, the British government had become fearful of Russell's pacifist activities. He was denied a passport, removed from his lectureship at Trinity College and banned from speaking in "prohibited areas" near the coast, presumably to stop him from signalling messages of peace to passing German submarines. (Actually to stop him from giving lectures to objectors in certain prison camps.)

I WROTE TO PRESIDENT WILSON OF AMERICA, ASKING HIM TO INTERVENE IN THE WAR AND PREVENT FURTHER BLOODSHED.

He also advised the young poet **Siegfried Sassoon** (1886-1967)...

I SERVED ON THE FRONT AND OBJECTED THAT THE WAR WAS CONTINUING FOR NO GOOD REASON.

But the war continued nonetheless. By 1916, most people realized that the casualty rates of troops on both sides were huge and unnecessary. But none of this seemed to dampen the civilian population's lust for war. Russell became increasingly depressed and misanthropic as a result: *"I hate the planet and the human race. I am ashamed to belong to such a species."*

Prison

Finally the authorities could take no more. Russell wrote an article which prophesied mass starvation in Europe and the occupation of Britain by the American Army who, he thought, would use violence to intimidate British workers who decided to strike. He was accused of writing an article likely to prejudice "His Majesty's relations with the United States of America" and was sent to prison for six months. He was a "first division" prisoner – able to furnish his cell, employ a cleaner, have flowers, books and food supplied on request.

*I INSISTED ON **THE TIMES** BEING DELIVERED EVERY DAY. PRISON LIFE WAS REMARKABLY CONGENIAL.*

He read Lytton Strachey's ironic debunking of "eminent" Victorians and mugged up on the relatively new but fast-expanding science of behaviourist psychology, and wrote a new book – *The Analysis of Mind* (1921).

Theories of Mind

Various theories of mind precede Russell's own. **Dualism**, probably the oldest of all, was made famous by philosophers like Plato and Descartes. Dualism argues that there are only two substances in the world — minds and physical objects.

MINDS ARE WHOLLY MENTAL AND NON-MATERIAL. PHYSICAL OBJECTS ARE WHOLLY MATERIAL AND NON-MENTAL.

HUMAN BEINGS THEREFORE ARE COMPOSED OF TWO SUBSTANCES - MINDS AND BODIES.

HOW IS IT, IF THESE TWO SUBSTANCES ARE WHOLLY DIFFERENT AND SEPARATE, THAT MINDS CAN AND DO INFLUENCE BODIES? HOW IS IT THAT MY MIND CAN MAKE MY FINGERS TYPE THIS SENTENCE?

The Idealist Theory of Mind

One obvious way out of Dualism's "Mind-Body" dilemma is to incorporate one of these two substances into the other. Idealism provides one solution.

The Materialist Answer

Materialists claim the opposite – everything that exists is physical, including minds. But this solution often requires a complicated redefinition of the term "physical".

Double Aspect Theory

An equally ingenious way out of the problem is often known as "Double Aspect" Theory. This claims that mental and physical events are really both properties of a deeper reality which itself is neither mental nor physical. The most famous advocate of this theory was the "monist" **Baruch Spinoza** (1632-77).

> THERE IS ONLY ONE SUBSTANCE IN "EVERYTHING" BECAUSE MINDS AND MATTER ARE ASPECTS OF THE SAME THING - GOD.

Hume was another kind of monist...

> WHEN WE TRY TO DETECT "MIND", ALL WE EVER FIND IS A COLLECTION OF IDEAS AND IMPRESSIONS. MATTER IS A FICTION WHICH WE INVENT IN ORDER TO IDENTIFY OUR SENSE IMPRESSIONS WITH HYPOTHETICAL PHYSICAL OBJECTS.

In the final analysis, matter and mind are rather similar kinds of entities, except that one transmits and the other receives.

Russell's Neutral Monism

Russell was greatly influenced by his prison readings of the American psychologist **William James** (1842-1910) who invented the term "neutral monism".

HUMAN EXPERIENCES CANNOT BE RIGIDLY CATEGORIZED AS EITHER MENTAL OR PHYSICAL, BECAUSE THEY ARE REALLY SOMETHING MYSTERIOUSLY IN BETWEEN.

I WROTE ABOUT MIND AND MATTER IN MY TWO BOOKS, THE ANALYSIS OF MIND (1921) AND THE SUBSEQUENT THE ANALYSIS OF MATTER (1927). ALL TALK OF MIND AND MATTER CAN BE REDUCED TO "EVENTS" - PHENOMENA WHICH ARE NEITHER INTRINSICALLY MATERIAL OR MENTAL.

By this time, Russell was well informed about modern atomic physics which is reluctant to talk about matter as "stuff" but thinks of it more in terms of "complicated systems of wave motions" or "events". As a radical empiricist, Russell was pleased to find that the scientific account of the physical world was quite unlike the "common sense" version.

Russell proceeded to show how unclear the concept of "mind" is. When our minds are active, "events" occur in our brains, which can be either mental, physical or both. The clearest example of this is in the act of perception. What we perceive is always impressions or sense-data. Russell maintains that these mysterious entities are themselves neither wholly mental or physical.

> *FOR EXAMPLE, COLOUR CAN BE ANALYSED BOTH BY A PSYCHOLOGIST AS AN OBJECT OF MENTAL EXPERIENCE AND BY A PHYSICIST AS A LIGHT-WAVE PHENOMENON.*

"COLOUR" IS THEREFORE NOT INTRINSICALLY EITHER A MENTAL OR A MATERIAL PHENOMENON.

Colour depends on its relation to other events and circumstances. So a physical object is really a set of appearances that radiate outwards – the mind is a receptor of these appearances – and sensations are a kind of physical event in the nervous system. Mind and matter are much less distinct than supposed.

Evaluation of Russell's Theory

Like other of Russell's philosophical views, it is an odd and complicated theory hard to accept at face value. How can mental phenomena like belief and desire be reduced to neutral and not wholly mental "events" in this sort of way? Not everyone was persuaded that modern scientific and traditional empiricist accounts of the world were as compatible as Russell thought.

NEVERTHELESS, IF YOU CAN ACCEPT RUSSELL'S VIEW THAT WE PERCEIVE THE WORLD VERY INDIRECTLY, IN OUR OWN BRAINS, AND THAT MATERIAL THINGS ARE ESSENTIALLY "EVENTS", THEN THE NEUTRAL MONIST THEORY MAY CONVINCE YOU.

And just because it goes against any common-sense view of us and the world, doesn't necessarily mean that it is wrong. (Even though nearly all contemporary philosophers, physicists or psychologists remain utterly unconvinced by it.)

A Satisfactory War

In some ways, Russell had a good war. He made many good friends and started an affair with a fellow protestor – Constance Malleson or "Colette O'Niel" which lasted for several years. In 1915, he also met the writer **D.H. Lawrence** (1885-1930). Lawrence was a passionate, intense and intolerant visionary who made a dramatic impression on Russell. Lady Ottoline was a fan and Russell was happy to join in the general chorus of approval.

LAWRENCE WAS A DIFFERENT KIND OF MISANTHROPE FROM RUSSELL.

HE WAS MORE OF A ROMANTIC REACTIONARY...

MOST 20TH-CENTURY INDIVIDUALS ARE INAUTHENTIC CREATURES REPRESSED BY AN INDUSTRIALIZED SOCIETY THAT VALUES RATIONAL AND MECHANISTIC THOUGHT PROCESSES ABOVE ALL ELSE AND EXCLUDES ALL TRUE HUMAN FEELINGS AND INSTINCTS.

Lawrence was supremely confident in himself and his ideas, and on the lookout for disciples, all of whom would live on a Pacific Island in a utopian commune called "Rananim". Surprisingly, Russell rather took to Lawrence, and, for a brief time, was deeply flattered by Lawrence's vows of eternal brotherhood.

IN MANY WAYS WE ARE WONDERFULLY ALIKE...

BUT...

I CAN'T MAKE HEAD NOR TAIL OF LAWRENCE'S PHILOSOPHY... IT IS NOT SYMPATHETIC TO ME.

A Bitter Turn

Not very surprisingly, the two fell out. Lawrence turned on Russell and wrote some letters that had a devastating effect on his former disciple.

Lawrence was perceptive enough to see that although Russell professed a philanthropic love for all mankind, in fact he was an isolated individual who disliked most of humanity and felt alienated from it.

Russell was a man who harboured deep suspicions about himself and his feelings.

WHEN LAWRENCE SPELT THEM OUT, I FELL INTO A STATE OF ALMOST SUICIDAL DESPAIR.

Lytton Strachey

Vanessa Bell

Fortunately, there were other less demanding visitors to Lady Ottoline's house like Aldous Huxley, Vanessa and Clive Bell, and Lytton Strachey who, no doubt, helped to cheer him up. He also began a brief and disastrous affair with the wife of the poet T.S. Eliot – Vivien Eliot.

113

Dora and the Russian Revolution

In 1917, Russell met the young feminist Dora Black who told him that she wanted children, but believed that fathers should have no rights over them. Russell came to think that he should abandon his several affairs and marry her. To begin with, Dora had reservations…

IF I CANNOT BE YOUR COMRADE, THEN IT IS NO USE LOVING YOU AT ALL.

Like many other radical intellectuals of the day, Dora and Bertie were excited by the news of the revolution in Russia. They supported the provisional government that replaced the autocratic regime of the Czar in 1917.

Russell believed that the new Russian model of Soviet-style "Councils", together with a reformed parliamentary democracy, was the best form of government.

Experience of Bolshevism

In 1920, Russell was invited to Russia – now under the control of Lenin's Bolshevik party – as a member of a delegation of trade unionists. Initially he still thought that "Socialists throughout the world should support the Bolsheviks and co-operate with them". But, unlike many of his comrades, Russell was unimpressed by what he saw. He had an instinctive dislike of the new collectivist ethic and criticized the new and supremely powerful centralized Bolshevik State which used oppression and violence to achieve its ends.

I FELT THAT EVERYTHING I VALUED IN HUMAN LIFE WAS BEING DESTROYED IN THE INTERESTS OF A GLIB AND NARROW PHILOSOPHY, AND THAT, IN THE PROCESS, UNTOLD MISERY WAS BEING INFLICTED UPON MANY MILLIONS OF PEOPLE.

The faithful Dora followed Russell into Russia but, like many left-wing British intellectuals, came back with a very different view from his of the new government. Whereas Russell saw "a close tyrannical bureaucracy, with a spy system more elaborate and terrible than the Czar's", Dora came away enthusiastic.

IN THE SOVIET UNION I HAD SEEN A VISION... OF THE MAKING OF A FUTURE CIVILIZATION.

LENIN SEEMS TO ME AN OPINIONATED PROFESSOR AND TROTSKY A VAIN ACTOR.

The Bolsheviks were imposing a rigid political regime with a secret police that ignored all basic human freedoms. Russell is often criticized for his political naivety, but in this instance he seems to have got things about right.

A Visit to China

Russell and Dora then went to China. Russell was both alarmed and gratified when his Chinese hosts treated him as a sage, and he responded with fulsome praise for Chinese civilization. Russell gave many lectures on social and political issues, one of which was attended by the young **Mao Tse-tung** (1883–1976), the future leader of Red China.

Although Russell continued to admire Chinese civilization then and for the rest of his life, he was shocked to see several examples of apparently callous disregard for the suffering of others.

He also fell dangerously ill of double pneumonia and nearly died there.

I WAS TOLD THAT THE CHINESE SAID THAT THEY WOULD BURY ME BY THE WESTERN LAKE AND BUILD A SHRINE TO MY MEMORY. I HAVE SOME REGRET THAT THIS DID NOT HAPPEN, AS I MIGHT HAVE BECOME A GOD, WHICH WOULD HAVE BEEN VERY CHIC FOR AN ATHEIST.

Shortly after his return to England, he divorced Alys and married an uneasy Dora (who thought she had betrayed her feminist principles by becoming a wife). Their first child – John Conrad Russell – arrived in 1921, and two years later they had a daughter, Kate.

119

Failure and Renewal

By the early 1920s, Russell had become a famous figure, both as a philosopher and as a commentator on current affairs. But he now had deep suspicions that Wittgenstein was right to believe that logic was really only a linguistic activity – merely a study of the structure of "empty" tautologies.

> *LOGIC CAN NO LONGER BE THE ANALYSIS OF DEEP AND PROFOUND TRUTHS ABOUT THE STRUCTURE OF REALITY – WHICH MEANS THAT THE LOGICIAN'S SEARCH FOR ETERNAL CERTAIN TRUTHS IS PROBABLY FUTILE.*

PRINCIPIA MATHEMATICA ?

It had also become clear how vulnerable the *Principia Mathematica* was to such criticisms. Russell's new enthusiasm was for science. He wrote several popular books for the ordinary reader on the new physics, and two more serious philosophical works on the foundations of science (*The Scientific Outlook* and *Human Knowledge, Its Scope and Limits*). It is to those that we must now turn.

Russell and Science

In his youth, Russell believed that rationality and science had the potential to solve all human problems. He saw the massive progress that modern science had made and confidently predicted that it would soon be "complete".

PHYSICAL SCIENCE IS APPROACHING THE STAGE WHERE IT WILL BE COMPLETE, AND THEREFORE UNINTERESTING.

RUSSELL'S OWN WORK ON MATHEMATICS AND LOGIC CONTRIBUTED A GREAT DEAL TO OUR UNDERSTANDING OF SCIENCE.

Philosophers could be useful to science by revealing what the fundamental metaphysical assumptions of science are – and by clarifying the meanings of crucial scientific terms like "cause", "law", "matter", and so on.

The New Physics

Russell was also a great reader of scientific books and articles. He was fascinated by the new nuclear physics and rather delighted by the fact that a great deal of modern science, like his own philosophy, turned out to be utterly **counter-intuitive**.

Russell also seized on the way that atomic physics seemed to eliminate the notion of "matter" and dissolve it into no more than "a series of events".

MY OWN RADICAL EMPIRICISM OF LOGICAL ATOMISM AND SOME OF THE CONCLUSIONS OF ATOMIC THEORY SEEM TO ME VERY SIMILAR.

Russell was also convinced that scientists were somehow more rational and disinterested than the majority of the population. This was why Russell came to believe that they were the best people to persuade governments to abandon nuclear weapons, as we'll see.

Philosophy and Science After Russell

Since Russell, philosophers of science led by **Thomas Kuhn** (b. 1922) and **Paul Feyerabend** (1924-94) have expressed grave doubts about what exactly science is and what kind of activity scientists are engaged in.

SCIENCE IS NOT QUITE THE VALUE-FREE "NEUTRAL" ACTIVITY THAT RUSSELL THOUGHT IT WAS.

MOST PHILOSOPHERS OF SCIENCE ARE NOWADAYS MORE "RELATIVIST" THAN RUSSELL WOULD HAVE ALLOWED.

THEY ALSO INSIST THAT EVEN SCIENTISTS' EXPERIENCES OF THE WORLD, HOWEVER IMMEDIATE OR DIRECT, ARE ALWAYS "THEORY LADEN".

We cannot help but impose categories (linguistic or otherwise) which mediate our experiences.

There is no pure, uncontaminated basic level of seeing that provides a guaranteed foundation for an empiricist programme of scientific knowledge. Other philosophers and psychologists now also argue that many of the central beliefs of traditional empiricist philosophy are false.

OUR EXPERIENCE OF THE WORLD AND THE OBJECTS IT CONTAINED COULD WELL BE QUITE DIRECT - IF FLAWED - AND THE WHOLE DOCTRINE OF "SENSE-DATA" A PHILOSOPHER'S FANTASY.

AND, AT A TIME WHEN MULTINATIONAL CORPORATIONS SEEM TO CONTROL MUCH OF **WHAT** SCIENTISTS STUDY AND **WHICH** OF THEIR RESULTS ARE PUBLISHED - WE DO NOT SHARE RUSSELL'S ABSOLUTE FAITH IN THE RATIONALITY AND ETHICAL PROBITY OF MOST SCIENTISTS.

The Beacon Hill Experiment

Russell had read a great deal about the new "Behaviourist" school of psychology during his stay in prison and became convinced that most human problems could be solved if people were prepared to grow up – to leave their primitive superstitions and irrational views behind and adopt a spirit of scientific scepticism. The key to human progress and happiness must lie in how children are educated – to be free of fear and stupidity. Russell and Dora thereby founded their famous Beacon Hill "free school" on the Sussex Downs.

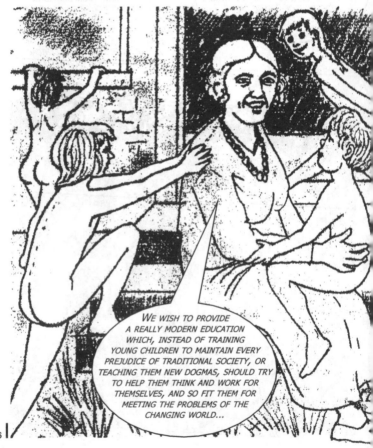

WE WISH TO PROVIDE A REALLY MODERN EDUCATION WHICH, INSTEAD OF TRAINING YOUNG CHILDREN TO MAINTAIN EVERY PREJUDICE OF TRADITIONAL SOCIETY, OR TEACHING THEM NEW DOGMAS, SHOULD TRY TO HELP THEM THINK AND WORK FOR THEMSELVES, AND SO FIT THEM FOR MEETING THE PROBLEMS OF THE CHANGING WORLD...

Children were allowed to choose which lessons they wanted to follow, given lots of healthy outdoor exercise, encouraged to lose their inhibitions about nudity and inspired academically. The school soon attracted a series of "problem children" from America which made everyday life there very challenging. It also acquired a certain notoriety. One highly unreliable story tells of a local Sussex vicar who came to visit…

OH MY GOD!

THERE IS NO GOD.

THE SCHOOL NEVER MADE ANY MONEY AND I HAD TO SUPPORT IT FROM MY OWN FUNDS FOR MANY YEARS.

OUR OWN CHILDREN HATED THE EXPERIENCE OF HAVING TO COPE WITH PARENTS WHO WERE ALSO TEACHERS.

Ironically, Russell's children grew up feeling as isolated as he himself had at Pembroke Lodge.

127

Sexual Freedom, Almost

Russell had already shocked those who believed in the official morality of the day. He wrote a very popular pamphlet which argued that Christianity was a religion of fear and blind obedience (*Why I Am Not a Christian*). Worse, he expressed views about sexual morality that were extremely unorthodox. He suggested (in *My Own View of Marriage*) that adultery was not necessarily always a particularly dreadful or destructive activity and (in *Marriage and Morals*) that conventional sexual morality was often damaging to all those who blindly accepted it, regardless of personal happiness. Russell and Dora very much practised what Russell preached. Dora seems to have been a wholly committed sexual pioneer.

I FREQUENTLY CRITICIZED MONOGAMY AND PATRIARCHY AND WAS QUITE OPEN ABOUT MY MANY OTHER RELATIONSHIPS.

I WAS RATHER LESS ENTHUSIASTIC ABOUT OUR OPEN MARRIAGE AND FINALLY REBELLED WHEN DORA HAD AN ILLEGITIMATE CHILD. I REJECTED HER RADICAL VIEWS ON COMPLETE SEXUAL FREEDOM.

In spite of this, Russell still had sexual relationships with two of his children's tutors and ended up marrying one of them – Patricia ("Peter") Spence – 40 years his junior. His eventual divorce from Dora was extremely acrimonious and the two of them were never reconciled. Dora remained committed to her feminist views.

I AM PERSUADED THAT INFIDELITIES ARE UNDESIRABLE SO LONG AS THE MARRIAGE HAS ANY REALITY.

I DON'T SEE WHY WE SHOULDN'T SLEEP AND COPULATE AS WE DAMN WELL PLEASE WITHOUT ECONOMIC AND EMOTIONAL SLAVERY TO FOLLOW.

The two were given joint custody of their children. From then on, Russell communicated with his ex-wife through his solicitor. He also lost interest in their great educational experiment, although Dora managed to keep the school going for several years afterwards.

Russell's Politics

In the 1920s and 30s, Russell's analytic and mathematical philosophies were influencing a whole new generation of young philosophers, especially the Logical Positivists. But by then, Russell had a new career – as a journalist, lecturer on popular subjects and author of books on science for the general reader (*ABC of Atoms, ABC of Relativity*). He went on several gruelling lecture tours in the United States and there pronounced on many different social issues – World Peace, Modern War, the British Labour Party and Russia.

I ALSO EXPLAINED HOW FASCISM AND COMMUNISM BOTH INFRINGE ON THE FREEDOM OF THE INDIVIDUAL – SOMETHING I BELIEVE ESSENTIAL FOR ANY CIVILIZED SOCIETY.

Russell was an old-fashioned liberal.

> "BY THIS I MEAN THAT, ON THE ONE HAND A MAN SHALL NOT BE PUNISHED EXCEPT BY DUE PROCESS OF LAW, AND ON THE OTHER HAND THAT THERE SHALL BE A SPHERE IN WHICH A MAN'S ACTIONS ARE NOT TO BE SUBJECT TO GOVERNMENTAL CONTROL. THIS SPHERE INCLUDES FREE SPEECH, A FREE PRESS AND RELIGIOUS FREEDOM."

Much of Russell's political writing is a continuing attempt to find a way of reconciling the need for some form of government authority with the greater need for personal freedoms. Russell distrusted governments of all kinds. He believed that those who sought power over others were often psychologically damaged. Russell wasn't much of a humanist either. He often felt isolated from his fellow human beings, and was frequently horrified by their stupid "herd mentality" and enthusiasm for war. But he wasn't wholly pessimistic about human nature – he thought most people had the potential for altruism but that societies rarely recognized this capacity and did little to nurture it.

The Anarchist View of Power

Russell's analysis of political society is similar to that of many anarchists who view all forms of government as an evil.

ALL TOO OFTEN IT IS AN APPETITE FOR POWER THAT DETERMINES HOW INDIVIDUALS RELATE TO EACH OTHER. POLITICAL AND SOCIAL INSTITUTIONS ARE USUALLY MALIGN REFLECTIONS OF THIS APPETITE.

KINGS RULE THROUGH FEAR AND CARE LITTLE FOR THE WELFARE OF MOST OF THEIR SUBJECTS.

EVENTUALLY THEIR POWER IS USURPED BY OLIGARCHIES OF VARIOUS KINDS - A WEALTHY ARISTOCRACY, LAND-OWNING GENTRY OR SOME FORM OF POLITICAL FACTION.

MODERN TOTALITARIAN DICTATORSHIPS ARE LIKE RELIGIONS WITH UNTHINKINGLY LOYAL DISCIPLES, CONVINCED BY A WORLD-PICTURE WHICH CLAIMS A MONOPOLY ON THE TRUTH.

THIS MAKES THEM INTOLERANT OF DISSENT AND UTTERLY INDIFFERENT TO THE HUMAN FREEDOMS THAT I VALUE SO HIGHLY.

Socialism and the State

Russell's experiences in Russia had made him deeply suspicious of State socialism. But he was also opposed to the concentration of economic power in the hands of individuals, powerful corporations or the State.

THAT'S WHY I CALL MYSELF A SOCIALIST – BUT ONE WHO BELIEVES THAT THE POWER OF THE STATE SHOULD BE REDUCED.

His solution lay in a British form of anarcho-syndicalism, usually known as "Guild Socialism", in which government was partly constituted by trade unions.

FACTORIES ELECT MANAGERS, ALL THE FACTORIES IN ONE INDUSTRY ARE FEDERATED INTO A GUILD, AND THIS CONTROLS THE CONDITIONS OF WORK AND SENDS DELEGATES TO A CONGRESS.

THE CONGRESS, TOGETHER WITH SOME FORM OF PARLIAMENT ELECTED BY CONSTITUENCIES, WOULD THEN BE THE ULTIMATE SOVEREIGN BODY.

Most people would then enjoy a reasonable standard of living and share in the government of the country. Power would never become too centralized.

The Threat of Nationalism

In his later political writings, Russell also warned of the great dangers of
nationalism, because it was very likely to provoke a third world war that
would destroy Western civilization for ever.

Devotion to the nation is perhaps the deepest and most widespread religion of the present age. Like the ancient religions, it demands its persecutions, its holocausts, its lurid, heroic cruelties; like them it is noble, primitive, brutal and mad.

All States encourage patriotic fervour which makes populations believe that
their nation is superior to all others. Some form of Internationalism is crucial
if civilization is to survive.

World Government

One of Russell's major political obsessions was the idea of a World Government given a monopoly over all weapons of mass destruction. Its military capacity would ensure that it could always enforce solutions to disputes between nations.

BUT HOW DOES THAT ACCORD WITH YOUR EARLIER CRITICISMS OF CENTRALIZED POWER?

I THINK IT IS A GRIM NECESSITY IF NUCLEAR WAR IS TO BE AVOIDED.

Russell believed that the only way a World Government could ever become a reality would be when one sovereign power – such as Russia or America – came to have dominance over the rest of the world. Hence, Russell thought America should threaten Russia with nuclear annihilation shortly after the Second World War – although he subsequently denied it.

Naïve About Politics

Russell didn't just theorize about politics. He stood for Parliament in 1907 (as a Women's Suffrage candidate), and twice in the 1920s (as a Labour Party candidate for Chelsea), but was never very committed to the views of any one political party. He soon became frustrated with the everyday world of political intrigue and grubby compromise. He became entitled to a seat in the House of Lords on the death of his elder brother Frank in 1931, but nearly all of his later political activities were extra-parliamentary and devoted to single-issue campaigns.

MANY OF HIS CONTEMPORARIES THOUGHT THAT RUSSELL WAS POLITICALLY VERY NAÏVE, AS THE HISTORIAN **G.M. TREVELYAN** (1876-1962) COMMENTED...

HE MAY BE A GENIUS IN MATHEMATICS... BUT ABOUT POLITICS HE IS A PERFECT GOOSE.

Not Completely a Goose

With hindsight, it's clear that Russell did say some silly things. But he was not a complete goose. He rejected the insane jingoism and mass slaughter of the First World War. He warned of the potential evil he saw in Bolshevism. He criticized America's involvement in Vietnam and warned everyone of the dangers of nuclear war. He thought America would emerge as the one great superpower to dominate the whole world.

138

The Prophet's Blind Spot

Russell often became extremely frustrated and bitter when people refused to comply with his vision of what the world should be like. The economist **J.M. Keynes** (1883-1946) noted the irony unseen by his visionary friend Russell.

BERTIE IN PARTICULAR SUSTAINED SIMULTANEOUSLY A PAIR OF OPINIONS, LUDICROUSLY INCOMPATIBLE. HE HELD THAT HUMAN AFFAIRS WERE CARRIED ON AFTER A MOST IRRATIONAL FASHION, BUT THAT THE REMEDY WAS QUITE SIMPLE AND EASY, SINCE ALL WE HAD TO DO WAS TO CARRY THEM ON RATIONALLY.

Scandal in America

Financial pressures forced Russell to accept teaching posts in the USA. In 1938, at the age of 66, he took his young wife with him and his new child, Conrad. He taught at the Universities of Chicago and California, and finally gained a professorship at the College of the City of New York. But the Episcopal Bishop of New York, a Dr William T. Manning, and a Mrs Jean Kay both protested at the scandalous appointment of a man who had openly advocated both atheism and adultery.

Russell seemed to have rather enjoyed the whole episode, especially as he was accused of the very same crimes that had condemned the Greek philosopher **Socrates** (c. 469-399 BC) to death in ancient Athens.

HE TOO WAS ACCUSED OF ATHEISM AND CORRUPTING THE YOUTH OF THE CITY.

HEMLOCK

His subsequent job at the eccentric "Barnes Foundation" in Philadelphia was initially more successful. The philanthropic millionaire Barnes paid Russell to give a series of lectures on the history of Western philosophy. Russell later turned these into his best-selling book which provided him with financial security for the rest of his life. But Barnes and he also came to disagree. Russell fled back to Trinity College where he had been offered a Fellowship. Russell certainly horrified many people by his "wicked atheism". So what were Russell's views on religion?

Russell and Religion

Russell lost his Christian faith at an early age but often admitted to mysterious spiritual longings. His emotional relationships with other people were frequently disappointing and he spent much of his life on a quest for emotional fulfilment and companionship. Russell also claimed to have had a personal epiphany on 10 February 1901. He saw Evelyn Whitehead – the wife of his collaborator A.N. Whitehead – in pain, and suddenly realized that...

THE LONELINESS OF THE HUMAN SOUL IS UNENDURABLE; NOTHING CAN PENETRATE IT EXCEPT THE HIGHEST INTENSITY OF THE SORT OF LOVE THAT RELIGIOUS TEACHERS HAVE PREACHED... IT FOLLOWS THAT WAR IS WRONG.

In 1923, he wrote *A Free Man's Worship* – a kind of gospel to agnosticism. It's a deeply felt, almost poetic work, which initially laments the fact that the universe, and so human life, are both ultimately doomed. If human beings need **something** to worship, he thinks, then they should celebrate goodness not power.

"I DO FEEL SOMETHING IN COMMON IN ALL THE GREAT THINGS... IT IS VERY MYSTERIOUS AND I REALLY DON'T KNOW WHAT TO THINK OF IT... BUT I FEEL IT IS THE MOST IMPORTANT THING IN THE WORLD AND REALLY THE ONE THING THAT MATTERS PROFOUNDLY. IT HAS MANY MANIFESTATIONS... LOVE... AND TRUTH..."

No Proof or Disproof of God

Russell had not lost his faith in Christianity but had long stopped believing in God.

THAT IS WHY HUMAN ACTIONS ARE IMPORTANT – BECAUSE GOD DOES NOT EXIST ALREADY... WHAT STRENGTH I NEED I MUST GET FROM MYSELF OR FROM THOSE WHOM I ADVISE.

He wrote several books in which he expressed strong anti-religious sentiments (*Why I Am Not a Christian* and *Mysticism and Logic*). He objected to religion on intellectual grounds – all the traditional philosophical "proofs" for God's existence were unconvincing. Nevertheless, for consistency's sake, he remained an agnostic, primarily because he admitted that he could never definitively **disprove** God's existence.

In *What I Believe*, Russell also argued that immortality was extremely unlikely.

He objected to orthodox religion on moral grounds. The Church had an unforgivable historical record of discouraging free enquiry. It inhibited social change and stood in the way of progress and the acquisition of knowledge. *"Works teaching that the earth moves round the sun remained on the Index of Prohibited Books until 1835."*

The Enemy of Christianity

Russell remained critical of all forms of organized religion throughout his life and rather enjoyed baiting Christians in his numerous books and articles, often very unfairly.

Russell in the Nuclear Age

The story of Russell's later years has little to do with philosophy. His journalistic output was prodigious and by now he was a popular broadcaster on the BBC. Whilst in America, Russell hadn't opposed the Second World War.

I AM STILL A PACIFIST IN THE SENSE THAT I THINK PEACE THE MOST IMPORTANT THING IN THE WORLD. BUT I DO NOT THINK THERE CAN BE ANY PEACE IN THE WORLD WHILE HITLER PROSPERS, SO I AM COMPELLED TO FEEL THAT HIS DEFEAT, IF AT ALL POSSIBLE, IS A NECESSARY PRELUDE TO ANYTHING GOOD...

But, on 6 August 1945, the Americans dropped the first atomic bomb on Hiroshima in Japan. Russell was one of the first to recognize what this meant. The so-called Cold War was already a reality and many people believed that a nuclear war between America and Russia was inevitable. Russell had no illusions about the Stalinist regime and rashly suggested that perhaps it would be a good thing if America went to war with Russia before it became a nuclear power itself.

The Peril of Nuclear Holocaust

Then, in 1949, Russia exploded its own atomic bomb. Next came the Korean War (1950-3) which opposed 16 UN Member States under US command to North Korean and Chinese Communist forces. This conflict stimulated Senator Joe McCarthy's anti-Communist witch-hunts in America. Russell quite genuinely believed that World War Three was a certainty.

I AM HAUNTED BY FEARS OF ATOMIC DEATH.

He went to the United States to issue warnings about the effects of McCarthyism on the whole country – America could no longer be the defender of democracy if it suppressed freedoms of expression.

The Nobel Prize

In 1950, Russell was awarded the Nobel Prize – not for his early mathematical philosophy but for literature – "in recognition for his varied and significant writings in which he champions humanitarian ideals and freedom of thought". In his acceptance speech, Russell warned his audience of the dangers of the primitive herd instinct in human beings.

Pugwash and CND

Warning humanity about the dangers of nuclear war occupied him for the rest of his life. Russell wrote to Einstein and other Nobel prize-winners to enlist their support. He became president of the famous "Pugwash" conferences which brought scientists together from both sides of the Cold War "Iron Curtain" to discuss the dangers of nuclear annihilation.

THE PUGWASH CONFERENCES WERE AWARDED THE NOBEL PEACE PRIZE IN 1995.

Then, in 1958, the Campaign for Nuclear Disarmament (CND) was founded in Britain, and Russell became its president.

THE CND MOVEMENT BELIEVES IN **UNILATERAL DISARMAMENT** - THAT BRITAIN SHOULD ABANDON ITS OWN NUCLEAR DETERRENT, AS AN EXAMPLE TO OTHER NATIONS.

Russell wrote such campaigning booklets for the movement as *Common Sense and Nuclear Warfare* and *Has Man a Future?*

Committee of 100

The controversial figure **Ralph Schoenman** now entered Russell's life. Schoenman was an American student who wanted to make CND a more radical political movement.

WE COULD INSTIGATE A PROGRAMME OF MASSIVE CIVILIAN RESISTANCE THAT WOULD OVERWHELM THE AUTHORITIES AND FORCE THEM TO CONCEDE.

SCHOENMAN PROMPTED THE COMMITTEE OF 100 – A GROUP OF PEOPLE WHO DECLARED THEIR WILLINGNESS TO GO TO JAIL IN SUPPORT OF CND.

Russell again became their president and joined in a famous sit-down protest outside the Ministry of Defence in 1961.

Russell explained why they were there on television.

IF THE PRESENT POLICIES OF THE WESTERN GOVERNMENTS ARE CONTINUED, THE ENTIRE HUMAN RACE WILL BE EXTERMINATED AND SOME OF US THINK THAT MIGHT BE RATHER A PITY.

Russell wrote many pamphlets and articles advocating British neutrality in the Cold War and finally found himself briefly in prison again for "inciting a breach of the peace". The Labour Party under **Hugh Gaitskill** (1906-63) rejected Unilateralism in 1960 and interest in the peace movement slowly died out.

Schoenman and the Prophet

Schoenman moved into the Russell household to become Russell's secretary. He was treated like Russell's own son. There is plenty of evidence to show that Schoenman flattered Russell in order to use him politically.

Russell and Schoenman became increasingly involved in the politics of Third World countries.

They supported the Cuban Revolution of 1959 and wrote letters to world leaders during the 1962 Cuban Missile Crisis.

Schoenman seems to have pushed Russell from a position of lofty neutrality into an alignment with Third World countries in their struggles against American influence. Further interventions followed – in the India–China border disputes and against the War in Vietnam.

The Bertrand Russell Peace Foundation was formed in order to promote world peace. The obstacle to world peace, as Russell and Schoenman saw it, was American world imperialism that could only be countered by world-wide local guerrilla movements.

IN 1966, I ANNOUNCED THE FORMATION OF THE INTERNATIONAL WAR CRIMES TRIBUNAL...

IT WAS SET UP TO INVESTIGATE AMERICAN ATROCITIES IN VIETNAM.

During this time, Schoenman was travelling all over the world in Russell's name, meeting with world leaders and impressing his and Russell's views upon them. He was finally deported back to America in 1968 and Russell's new wife Edith managed to persuade the 97-year-old prophet that Schoenman was no longer worthy of support.

HE USED MY REPUTATION TO SUPPORT HIS OWN VIEWS. AND HE HAD A VASTLY INFLATED OPINION OF MY IMPORTANCE.

The Viper

The accepted view of Schoenman is of a "viper" in the Russell household –
a kind of hypnotic Svengali figure who manipulated a naïve Russell into
stating extremist left-wing political views that were actually Schoenman's
own. But the truth is probably more complex. For a long time, Russell had
despised Western governments and his own pronouncements were
frequently radical and anarchistic.

BUT MUCH OF WHAT HE SAID DOESN'T SOUND *THAT* EXTREME...

THE CUBAN CRISIS VERY NEARLY DID ESCALATE INTO WORLD WAR III.

THE AMERICAN INTERVENTION IN VIETNAM WAS A DREADFUL MISTAKE.

AND NUCLEAR WEAPONS STILL REMAIN A THREAT EVEN TODAY.

Russell seems to have been quite content for Schoenman to draft
manifestos and issue various kinds of political pamphlets in his name
– and was quite happy to defend them when challenged.

Towards the end, his life was necessarily that of a private individual and he was content for Schoenman to act out his continuing existence as a public figure on the world stage. Russell undoubtedly enjoyed hearing his praises sung and his world influence celebrated. The real innocent, in a sense, was Schoenman himself who believed in the myth of Russell, the "International World Statesman", and occasionally made a complete idiot of himself in several of his "missions" to Third World countries.

The Closing Years

Russell's children by then were well into adult life. His daughter Kate was married and living in the USA. His second son Conrad was about to become a successful academic historian. Russell and Patricia had separated. He spent a great deal of time trying to help his first son John, who oscillated between his and Dora's households and was eventually diagnosed as schizophrenic.

In 1952, Russell married Edith Finch, an American academic whom Russell had known for several years. It was at this time that he finished writing his *Autobiography* which, he insisted, could only be published after his death.

In 1953, the Russell personal family history repeated itself.

The End

Russell had lived to be a very old man. His public persona still made internationally recognized pronouncements on world affairs but the private man was increasingly deaf and not always able to follow other people's conversations. He was well aware that his body was giving way.

He was finally reconciled with his second son, Conrad, in 1968, but never with his first, John. Russell died of bronchitis on 2 February 1970 and his ashes were scattered on the Welsh hills.

Assessments of Russell's Work

Russell published a huge amount of philosophical work, some of which, like Logical Atomism and Neutral Monism, is no longer very influential. But there's little doubt that Russell's work drastically changed the direction and subject matter of Western philosophy for ever.

PRINCIPIA MATHEMATICA TRIED TO REDEFINE THE FUNDAMENTAL PRINCIPLES OF MATHEMATICS ON A FEW BASIC LAWS OF LOGIC.

THE WHOLE MASSIVE PROJECT MAY HAVE BEEN MISCONCEIVED AND A GRAND FAILURE...

BUT IT HELPED TO MAKE MODERN LOGIC THE POWERFUL ANALYTICAL TOOL THAT IT IS TODAY.

Alfred Tarski   W.V.O. Quine   Saul Kripke

Modern Logicians like **Alfred Tarski** (1902-83) owe a huge debt to the pioneering work of Russell and Whitehead, and many modern philosophers like **W.V.O. Quine** (b. 1908), **Saul Kripke** (b. 1940), **Donald Davidson** (b. 1917) and **Michael Dummett** (b. 1925) make logic one of their central philosophical concerns.

Philosophical Descendants

Russell was partly and unwittingly responsible for the birth of several new schools of philosophy. One was the Logical Positivists. This group (the Vienna Circle) accepted his radical empiricist programme, his advocacy of science and his belief in the power of logical analysis to disentangle the confusions of ordinary language into true "logical form".

WITH THESE TOOLS, WE DEVELOPED A RADICAL NEW THEORY OF MEANING CALLED **VERIFICATIONISM**.

Moritz Schlick
(1882-1936)

Rudolf Carnap
(1891-1970)

Friedrich Waismann
(1896-1959)

ALL MEANINGFUL, I.E. **VERIFIABLE**, PROPOSITIONS (EXCEPT THOSE OF MATHS AND LOGIC) HAVE TO REFER SPECIFICALLY TO SENSE-DATA OR BE EMPIRICALLY TESTABLE IN SOME SENSE.

ANYTHING NOT VERIFIABLE - LIKE MUCH METAPHYSICAL SPECULATION - WE CONTEMPTUOUSLY DISMISS AS "NONSENSE".

The British philosopher **A.J. Ayer** (1910-89), in *Language, Truth and Logic* (1936), introduced this doctrine from Austria and its influence on English philosophy was considerable. Logical Positivists soon found, however, that the "Verification Principle" itself was untestable – as was a great deal of cutting-edge physics.

NO ONE HAS YET SEEN A "QUARK" AND YET ATOMIC PHYSICISTS SEEM QUITE HAPPY WITH THEM AND DO NOT CONSIDER THEMSELVES TO BE TALKING NONSENSE.

AND NOT MANY PHILOSOPHERS NOWADAYS ACCEPT THAT MEANING IS DERIVED FROM EMPIRICAL VERIFICATION...

YET, SOME LOGICAL POSITIVISTS DID BELIEVE, AS I DO, IN RUSSELL'S POSSIBILITY OF A PURE LOGICAL AND ATOMISTIC LANGUAGE BASED ON SENSE-DATA.

Such a language would be non-inferential and bring a new rigour to scientific observations and methodology. But no convincing attempt has ever been made to devise such a language, and few scientists now believe it would be very helpful.

The Linguistic Analysis School

Russell's early work also influenced the "analytic" or "linguistic" school of philosophy which, until very recently, defined what the activity of philosophy meant – "thinking about thinking".

Gilbert Ryle (1900-76)

*RUSSELL'S ESSAY **ON DENOTING** WITH ITS ACCOMPANYING "THEORY OF DESCRIPTIONS" LED SOME OF US TO BELIEVE THAT THE PRIMARY FUNCTION OF PHILOSOPHY WAS TO DISSECT AND ANALYSE **CONCEPTS**, RATHER THAN ENGAGE IN METAPHYSICAL SPECULATION.*

AND THIS IS WHAT MANY BRITISH AND AMERICAN PHILOSOPHERS PROCEEDED TO DO THROUGHOUT THE POST-WAR YEARS.

J.L. Austin (1911-1960)

P.F. Strawson (b. 1919)

CONCEPTUAL OR LINGUISTIC ANALYSIS WAS ALSO ENCOURAGED BY THE LATER WORK OF WITTGENSTEIN...

Some philosophers in the "Oxford School" – **Gilbert Ryle** (1900-76), **J.L. Austin** (1911-1960), **P.F. Strawson** (b. 1919) and others – maintained that this was virtually all that philosophy had left to do. Most philosophical "problems" were illusory and could be efficiently "dissolved" by a close analysis of how previous philosophers had misused language and been misled into "category mistakes".

The Deeper Aim of Philosophy

Russell admired the Logical Positivist programme of reform, because of its radical empiricist approach and its belief in logical analysis. But he could never accept the view that philosophy is merely linguistic analysis. This is why he thought that much of the later philosophy of Wittgenstein was essentially "trivial". For Russell, analysis was only a means to a loftier end.

CLARIFICATION IS NECESSARY IF WE ARE TO FULLY COMPREHEND WHAT WE ARE SAYING ABOUT REALITY AND HOW THINGS ARE...

BUT LINGUISTIC ANALYSIS SHOULD NEVER BE AN END IN ITSELF - THE ENDLESS SHARPENING OF A SET OF TOOLS THAT ARE NEVER USED.

For Russell, philosophy was always to be a more serious activity – an attempt to understand the true nature of reality and ourselves. He insisted that there were still many important philosophical questions left to be answered and that their answers could be discovered if you were prepared to work away at them hard enough.

The Failure of Empiricism

Russell is famous for continually qualifying his earlier work. One obvious reason for this was his attempt to make empiricism the sole foundation for different theories of meaning and metaphysics – a task for which it now seems wholly inappropriate. It also helps to explain why many of his works of "pure" philosophy are a difficult read.

THEY ARE RIGOROUS ATTEMPTS TO SHOW **HOW** THE EMPIRICIST PROGRAMME MIGHT BE FORCED TO ACCOMPLISH THESE TASKS.

RUSSELL MAY BE THE LAST GREAT PHILOSOPHER TO BELIEVE THAT IT IS STILL POSSIBLE TO ESTABLISH DEMONSTRABLE AND INDUBITABLE KNOWLEDGE. BUT HE FAILED TO DO IT.

Most modern philosophers now say that he set himself inherently impossible tasks – so they are quite happy to limit themselves to yet more investigations into language and meaning. In his 1948 book, *Human Knowledge, Its Scope and Limits*, Russell sadly and finally agreed that there probably is no such thing as certain knowledge.

Nevertheless, Russell discovered the work of Frege and helped to bring it to the attention of all English-speaking philosophers. He encouraged Wittgenstein. He was the father of the Vienna Circle and the unwilling god-father of analytical philosophy – much of which is still taught in most British universities. He insisted on the importance of philosophy and science to each other. He revolutionized logic and our understanding of mathematics. And, although he probably never realized it, Russell was one of the founders of this modern computer age.

Russell, the Intellectual Icon

Russell was a sort of naïve English equivalent of **Voltaire** (1694-1778) – a passionate rationalist who was outraged by all the examples he saw of irrational belief and needless cruelty. He was an unusual British phenomenon – an intellectual who made pronouncements about contemporary life and current affairs to whom ordinary people listened with respect (much to the distress of governments). In the popular imagination, he was the man with an enormous brain, who therefore had the right to speak out and be listened to – even if most political and social problems are not very amenable to his kind of logical analysis. Towards the end of his life, Russell became an iconic figure for the young. They read his populist books, listened to his broadcasts on the radio and saw him on television. Russell helped set the tone for future protests and encouraged young people to challenge entrenched political and social ideologies. He had no respect for authority and encouraged everyone to share his distrust of conventional politics and politicians. And for this alone many people will remain forever grateful.

"I MAY HAVE THOUGHT THE ROAD TO A WORLD OF FREE AND HAPPY HUMAN BEINGS SHORTER THAN IT IS PROVING TO BE... NEVERTHELESS, MANY (OF US) STILL SHARE THE PURSUIT OF A VISION, BOTH PERSONAL AND SOCIAL. PERSONAL: TO CARE FOR WHAT IS NOBLE, FOR WHAT IS BEAUTIFUL, FOR WHAT IS GENTLE: TO ALLOW MOMENTS OF INSIGHT TO GIVE WISDOM AT MORE MUNDANE TIMES. SOCIAL: TO SEE IN IMAGINATION THE SOCIETY THAT IS TO BE CREATED, WHERE INDIVIDUALS GROW FREELY AND WHERE HATE AND GREED AND ENVY DIE BECAUSE THERE IS NOTHING TO NOURISH THEM."

Bertrand Russell wrote an astonishing number of books, pamphlets, articles and letters. All of Russell's political and social philosophy is impeccably written in straightforward prose. Much of his academic philosophy is rather more demanding. Nearly all of his important works are still in print. It isn't possible to list everything, but here are all the works referred to in this book.

1903 **The Principles of Mathematics** (Routledge, 1992)
1910-13 **Principia Mathematica** (Cambridge University Press, 1927;
   Abridged Vol. I: *Principia Mathematica to *56*, Cambridge University Press, 1997).
   Even Whitehead, the joint author, confessed to Russell that when he read the *Principia Mathematica*, he was "in a fog as to where you are". So, to all those who make the attempt to read this great philosophical monument, one can only say, "Good Luck!"
1912 **The Problems of Philosophy** (Oxford University Press, 2001)
1914 **Our Knowledge of the External World** (Routledge, 1993)
1915 **The Ethics of War** (*International Journal of Ethics*, vol. 25, Jan 1915, pp. 127-42)
1918 **Roads to Freedom** (Routledge, 1996)
1918 **The Philosophy of Logical Atomism** (Open Court Publishing Group, 1985)
1918 **Mysticism and Logic** (Routledge, 1986)
1921 **The Analysis of Mind** (Routledge, 1989)
1923 **A Free Man's Worship** (Routledge, 1986)
1923 **The ABC of Atoms** (Kegan Paul, 1923)
1925 **What I Believe** (Kegan Paul, 1925; repr. in *Why I Am Not a Christian, and Other Essays on Religion and Related Subjects*, Simon & Schuster, 1967)
1925 **The ABC of Relativity** (Routledge, 1997)
1926 **On Education** (Routledge, 1985)
1927 **The Analysis of Matter** (Routledge, 1992)
1927 **Why I Am Not a Christian** (Routledge, 1975)
1928 **My Own View of Marriage** (*Outlook*, vol. 148, 7 Mar 1928, pp. 376-7)
1929 **Marriage and Morals** (Routledge, 1985)
1931 **The Scientific Outlook** (Routledge, 2001)
1945 **A History of Western Philosophy** (Routledge, 2000)
1948 **Human Knowledge: Its Scope and Limits** (*Human Knowledge: Its Scope and Value*, Routledge, 1992)
1955 **Why I Took to Philosophy** (Radio talk, reprinted in *Basic Writings*, see below)
1959 **My Philosophical Development** (Routledge, 1985)
1959 **Common Sense and Nuclear Warfare** (Routledge, 2001)
1961 **Has Man a Future?** (Spokesman Books, 2001)
1967, 1968, 1969 **The Autobiography of Bertrand Russell** (Routledge, 2001)

Most of Russell's most famous essays can also be found in collections:

Sceptical Essays (Routledge, 1985)
In Praise of Idleness (Routledge, 1984)
The Basic Writings of Bertrand Russell, 1903-1959 (Routledge, 1992)
The Selected Letters of Bertrand Russell: The Public Years, 1914-1970 (Routledge, 2001)

Russell sold nearly all of his manuscripts to MacMaster University, Toronto, and they are presently producing a lengthy series of volumes containing nearly all of Russell's shorter works: **The Collected Papers of Bertrand Russell.**

A large number of Russell's shorter works, including the famous **On Denoting**, can also be tracked down on the World Wide Web, as any competent search engine will quickly reveal. (A good place to start would be www.mcmaster.ca/russdocs/russell1.htm.)

It should come as no surprise to find that there are also many books *about* Russell:

Bertrand Russell, the Passionate Skeptic, by Alan Wood (Simon & Schuster, 1958), is an enthusiastic account of Russell's life, if inevitably incomplete.

Bertrand Russell in two volumes, **The Spirit of Solitude, 1872-1921** and **The Ghost of Madness, 1921-1970**, by Ray Monk (Vintage, 1997, 2000). This is the most recently published and most exhaustive biography of Russell. The first volume is very well researched and sympathetic to its subject. Unusually, Ray Monk tries to explain Russell's philosophical development as well as delineating his very complicated life. This means he makes a brave attempt to explain the complex intricacies of **Principia Mathematica** to the general reader, for which this writer remains extremely grateful. Volume Two gets rather bogged down in the gruesome details of Russell's (mostly disastrous) family life and the author seems impatient with most of Russell's political journalism. Nevertheless, both books are excellent.

Books on Russell's philosophy are, of necessity, not always an easy read:

Bertrand Russell, by John Watling (Oliver and Boyd, 1970), is a reasonably accessible book for the beginner.
Russell, by A.J. Ayer (University of Chicago Press, 1972), is a sympathetic account of Russell's philosophy by a fellow empiricist, but not always an easy read.
Russell's Theory of Knowledge, by Elizabeth Eames (Routledge, 1992), is useful, but again not easy.
Bertrand Russell and the British Tradition in Philosophy, by D.E. Pears (Random House, 1967), provides a more detailed explanation of Russell's Logical Atomism and reveals its debt to the work of Hume and Wittgenstein.

Other books that this writer found useful are:

Why Does Language Matter to Philosophy?, by Ian Hacking (Cambridge University Press, 1975), looks in some detail at Russell's disastrous atomist theory of meaning.
Theories of the Mind, by Stephen Priest (Penguin, 1991), examines Russell's philosophy of mind.
Pi in the Sky, by John D. Barrow (Clarendon Press, 1992), describes and evaluates Russell's logicist ambitions for mathematics.

And any book about Russell inevitably has to recommend at least two books about Wittgenstein, whose philosophy was, however unwittingly, often a series of ripostes to Russell's own:

Ludwig Wittgenstein, by David Pears (Harvard University Press, 1986).
Introducing Wittgenstein, John Heaton and Judy Groves (Icon Books, 1999).

About the Author and Artist

Dave Robinson has taught philosophy to students for many years. He is the author of several Icon "Introducing" books on Ethics, Descartes, Plato and Rousseau. He has also contributed to the Icon "Postmodern Encounters" series with a book on Nietzsche and Postmodernism. He lives in Devon, with his partner and a very spoilt cat.

Judy Groves has worked on many of the Icon "Introducing" series, including *Wittgenstein*, *Philosophy*, *Plato* and *Aristotle*. She also teaches illustration.

Acknowledgements

The author would like to thank Richard Appignanesi for editing an unwieldy manuscript into something more incisive and elegant, and he is much impressed by the wit and craft of the illustrator, Judy Groves, who has made this book much less daunting to its readers than it otherwise might have been. He is also grateful to his partner Judith who has spent many happy hours patiently listening to his interminable late-night accounts of Logical Atomism without subsequently suing for divorce.

The artist would like to thank David King for the loan of photographs from his collection and Dave Robinson for his help in tracking down visual reference. Thanks also to Amy Groves.

Index